Japanese Stems & Nuances

The Essential Guide to How Japanese Really Works

Japanese Stems & Nuances

The Essential Guide to How Japanese Really Works

Edgar J. Hern

Published by Clarity House Publications
Ontario, California, USA

First Edition: April, 2026

10 9 8 7 6 5 4 3 2

Printed in the United States of America
Times New Roman, 11

Cover design: Edgar J. Hern

All Japanese example sentences, romaji transcriptions, English translations, and explanatory notes in this book are original and were created specifically for this work. No external sources were quoted or adapted.

X: @EdgarJHern12748

Publisher's Cataloging-in-Publication Data
Names: Hern, Edgar J. 1959-, author.
Title: Japanese stems and nuances : the essential guide to how Japanese really works / Edgar J. Hern, editor.
Description: Includes index. | Las Vegas, NV: KDP, 2026.
Identifiers: LCCN: 2026908127 | ISBN: 979-8-9954685-0-9 (paperback).
Subjects: LCSH Japanese Language-Grammar.| BISAC LANGUAGE STUDY / Japanese
Classification: LCC PL523 .K58 H47 2026 | DDC 495.6--dc23

CONTENTS

INTRODUCTION

Congratulations on embarking upon the journey of learning a new language. Learning Japanese is challenging enough, but mastering the stems and nuances that shape its structure will unlock the deeper meaning behind every sentence. *Japanese Stems and Nuances* will dispel any doubts or concerns that may arise, guiding you toward clarity and confidence in this fascinating language.

Going forward, readers are expected to have already mastered hiragana and katakana, along with basic vocabulary such as family terms, numbers, and colors, as well as the foundational verbs いる (iru) "to exist (animate)" and ある (aru) "to exist (inanimate)." These existence verbs are usually introduced early in Japanese study. (Note: いる written as 要る, though pronounced the same, appears in Part 1 as the verb meaning "to need" or "to require.")

思う (omou) "to think" and 知る (shiru) "to know" are usually introduced early in a learner's journey, so they don't need much spotlight in a book about stems and nuance. However, unlike omou and shiru, kanjiru 感じる is often under-emphasized in beginner and even intermediate materials, despite being central to how Japanese expresses subjective experience. Learners may know how to say "I think" (omou) or "I know" (shiru), but they often struggle to naturally say "I feel" (kanjiru), especially in subtle contexts like emotions, atmosphere, or impressions. Kanjiru is covered in depth in Part VI: Voice & Agency.

Because these fundamentals are assumed knowledge, this book will not review them. Instead, it will focus on expanding your vocabulary and taking your skills to the next level. By "skills," I mean strengthening your command of sentence tenses, mastering the kanji for each new word, and learning how to apply nuances naturally in speech. Think of this book as an intensive crash course designed to sharpen your Japanese expression.

Japanese Stems and Nuances is broken into three sections. Part one introduces stems and nuances that are used either by itself or attached to other words. Japanese "stems" and suffixes don't behave uniformly — some target verbs, some adjectives, some nouns. That's why mastering them gives you the nuance you're chasing: each one reshapes the sentence's emotional or logical flow. Plenty of sentence structures will be given to help clarify the stem word, while introducing a list of new vocabulary words.

It will help to learn the vocabulary introduced in each section, as this will make it easier to follow the Japanese example sentences throughout the book. To save you the time and disruption of looking up unfamiliar words in a dictionary, each sentence is presented in a three-line format: Japanese, romaji, and English. Within that structure, key vocabulary is highlighted using **bold**, underline, and boxed formatting so you can instantly match each word across all three lines. This system allows you to read fluidly, stay focused on nuance, and build vocabulary naturally as you progress.

To reinforce everything you learn in these eight sections, a comprehensive quiz appears at the end of the book. It is designed not as a test of memorization, but as a way to deepen your intuition: recognizing stems in context, feeling the nuance they add, and choosing the form that best matches the speaker's intention. By the time you reach it, you will have encountered every pattern multiple times in natural sentences, so the quiz becomes a final pass that strengthens your confidence and solidifies your understanding.

Throughout this book, you will see notes that are indented to different levels (nested indentation). This is intentional. A single indent marks a general note or clarification. A deeper indent indicates a secondary point or a related nuance worth exploring. These indents also create open space in the left margin, giving you room to write your own notes, reminders, or examples as you study.

PART I: ASSERTION & EMPHASIS

Key stems and nuances in this section:

- bakari ばかり, dake だけ (when used emphatically, "nothing but / only")
- koso こそ → Strong focus/emphasis ("this very thing")
- nante なんて → emotional emphasis, highlights speakers attitude
- tte って → Quotation, colloquial emphasis
- sa さ, yo よ, ze ぜ, zo ぞ → Strong assertion, masculine tone, casual emphasis

Vocabulary to review:

amai	甘い	sweet
ashita	明日	tomorrow
asobu	あそぶ	to play
bakari	ばかり	only, nothing but
benkyō	勉強	study
bikkuri	びっくり	surprised
chairo	茶色	brown
eiga	映画	movie
fuku	服	clothes, outfit
gaishutsu	外出	going out
ganbaru	頑張る	to do one's best; to try hard; to persist; to hang in there
hanashi	話	story
hashiru	走る	to run
heya	部屋	room, space
hito	人	person, someone, anyone / people (as a group) / one (the only one) / personnel, etc.
honki	本気	seriously
hontō or honto	ほんとう or ほんと	really, truly
iru	要る	to need / to require
iru	いる	to exist / to be (living things)
issho	一緒	together
kakugo	覚悟	mental readiness / resolve / preparedness for what's coming
kami	神	God
kangaeru	考える	to think
karakau	からかう	to tease, to make fun of

katsu	勝つ	win
kazoku	家族	family
keshiki	景色	scenery, view
ki	気	refers to internal state, mental focus, emotional energy, or intention
kiku	聞く	to listen, to hear
kiku	訊く	to ask (a question)
kiku	利く	to be effective
koe	声	voice
kotoba	言葉	words, language, speech, or expression
kuruma	車	car
makeru	負ける	lose
mijikai	短い	short
mondai	問題	problem, question (an issue that needs to be addressed)
niwa	庭	garden
ochitsuku	落ち着く	to calm down / to feel settled
okane	お金	money
okashi	お菓子	sweets
okureru	遅れる	to be late, to fall behind, to be delayed, to miss (an event / transport)
ore	俺	I (first-person pronoun)
osoi	遅い	slow
otoshi	落とし	drop
rashii	らしい	It seems
ryūgaku	留学	study abroad
saifu	財布	wallet
saikin	最近	recently, lately
shiawase	幸せ	happiness, good fortune
shigoto	仕事	work
shinjiru	信じる	to believe, to trust
shippai	失敗	failure
sugoku	すごく	very, really, extremely, so much
susumu	進む	to advance, to move forward, to proceed
taberu	食べる	to eat
taido	態度	attitude
taisetsu	大切	important, to value

tomodachi	友だち	friend
torinaosu (compound verb)	取り直す	to pull yourself together / to start over / to reset your mindset
toru	取る	to take / to pick up / to grab / to get
uru	売る	sell
utsukushii	美しい	beautiful, lovely
yaru	やる	to do, to perform, to carry out, to try, to give (casual)
yasai	野菜	vegetables
yasashii	優しい	gentle, kind, sweet, affectionate
yasumi	休み	holiday
yatta	やった	I/He/She/They/We did it!
yomichi	夜道	a dark road

Diving further into the stems and nuances

Bakari ばかり:

A multifunctional word meaning things like:

- "only / just"
- "nothing but"
- "just did (recently)"
- "always doing / doing too much of"
- "about / approximately" (older / limited use)

Its nuance depends on the grammar pattern it appears in.

Pattern 1: The most common meaning is "only / just / nothing but / all you ever do is." It expresses limitation, that something is restricted to one thing.

Structure:

- Noun + ばかり
- Verb dictionary form + ばかり
- Verb て-form + ばかり

Examples:

Kanojo wa yasai bakari taberu.

彼女は野菜ばかり食べる。

She eats only vegetables.

Ano **mise** wa okashi bakari uru.
あの店は お菓子 ばかり売る。
That **shop** sells nothing but sweets.

Asobi bakari shite iru.
遊びばかりしている。
He does nothing but **play**.

This form often carries a slightly complaining tone when used about people's habits.

Pattern 2: Expresses recent completion "just did / just finished doing." In this nuance, ばかり is more subjective than "tatokoro" たところ ("just now"). It implies the speaker feels it was recent.

Structure:

- Verb (past tense) + ばかり

Examples:
Tabeta bakari desu.
食べたばかりです。
I just **ate**.

Kita bakari na no ni, mō kaeru **no**?
来たばかりなのに、もう帰る**の**？
You just got here — and you're leaving already?

Note: The Question Marker の vs. か:
In mō kaeru no? (もう帰るの？), the の at the end is a casual question marker. It's different from か, which is the standard polite question ending.

Here's the contrast:
1. の (casual, emotional, seeking explanation)
Sentence-final の？ adds: curiosity, softness, emotional involvement, "What's the reason?" feeling, or a sense of seeking explanation, not just information.
It's very common in casual speech, especially when reacting to something unexpected.
→ nuance: Why so soon? What's going on?
It's not just a question — it's a question with feeling.

2. か (polite, neutral, formal)

Sentence-final か is: polite, neutral, information-seeking, emotionally flat, and is used in formal or polite contexts

Example:
Mō kaerimasu ka.
もう帰りますか。
Are you going home now?
→ neutral, polite, no emotional shading.

Pattern 3: This pattern expresses excessive repetition or habitual behavior, usually with a negative or complaining nuance. The nuance here is, "All you ever do is…" "You're always doing…" "You do this too much." It is often used to scold, complain, or express frustration.

Structure:

- Verb (て-form) + ばかり + いる

Gēmu shite bakari iru.
ゲームしてばかりいる。
He's always playing **games** / All he ever does is play **games**.

Nete bakari ita.
寝てばかりいた。
I did nothing but **sleep**.

Hanashite bakari iru.
話してばかりいる。
They're always **talking**.

Note: Pattern 3 looks similar to Pattern 1, but it is different. The difference is structural and semantic.

Pattern 1

- ばかり attaches to a noun, dictionary verb, or て-form.
- It expresses limitation: "only / just / nothing but."

Pattern 3

- ばかり attaches specifically to Verb-て + いる.
- It expresses excessive repetition: "always doing / doing too much." They feel similar because both can describe habits. But the grammar and nuance are different:

Part I: Assertion & Emphasis

P1	Noun / Verb + ばかり	"only / just / nothing but"	sometimes complaining
P3	Verb-て + ばかり + いる	"always doing / doing too much"	strongly complaining / scolding

Pattern 1 describes a state of limitation.
Pattern 3 describes a continuous, repeated action.

Pattern 4: This pattern emphasizes that something is filled with or covered in one type of thing. It's more visual or physical than Pattern 1. The nuance here is "full of ___" "nothing but ___ everywhere" "packed with ___". It often describes a scene, place, or situation.

Structure:

- Noun + ばかり

Examples:
Kono **heya** wa gomi bakari da.
この**部屋**はゴミばかりだ。
This **room** is full of trash.

Koko wa hito bakari.
ここは人ばかり。
This place is packed with people.

Kaban no naka wa **kami** bakari.
カバンの中は**紙**ばかり。
My bag is full of **papers**.

Pattern 5: This is a more formal or literary use. It appears in writing, older speech, or set expressions. The nuance here is "about / roughly / approximately." It is softer and more old-fashioned than goro ごろ (around) or kurai くらい (about).

Structure: Number / amount + ばかり
Examples:
Sanjuppun bakari **matte** kudasai.
30分ばかり**待って**ください。
Please **wait** about 30 minutes.

Kore bakari no koto.
こればかりのこと。
This is the only thing. / It's nothing more than this.

Note: In "kore bakari no koto," the phrase no koto turns the preceding words into an abstract idea — "the matter of ~ / the thing about ~." Here it softens and generalizes kore bakari ("only this"), giving the sense of "this sort of thing" or "just this matter." A full explanation of no koto appears in Part VIII: OTHER IMPORTANT WORDS.

Hyakuen bakari katta.
100円ばかり買った。
I bought about 100 yen's worth.

Dake だけ:

A particle that functions as "only / just / as much as." だけ limits or restricts the amount, number, or scope of something. Think of it as drawing a small circle around something and saying: "Only this. Nothing more."

1) Core meaning: "only / just." This is the most common use.

Kyou wa jikan ga nai kara, **pan** dake tabeta.
今日は時間がないから、パンだけ食べた。
I didn't have time today, so I only ate **bread**. Or,
Because I didn't have time today, I only ate bread.
Here, だけ limits the food to "bread and nothing else."

Note: Why から can also be translated as "so." English prefers to put the result first:
I didn't have time today, so I only ate bread.
Even though から means "because," the natural English translation often uses "so" because English likes cause → effect, not effect → cause.

2) だけ with verbs: "as much as / as far as." When だけ attaches to a verb in dictionary form, it means: "as much as you want / as far as you can / to your heart's content."

Suki na dake **totte** ii yo.
好きなだけ**取って**いいよ。
You can **take** as much as you like.
Here, だけ expresses extent, not "only."

Note: totte (取って) is the て-form of toru (取る – to take). Here, 取って connects to いい to form the permission pattern ～ていい, meaning "it's okay to do X" / "you may do X."

3) ～だけで: "just by / simply by." When だけ combines with で, it forms a new pattern: だけで = just by doing / simply by / with only.

Anata no **koe** o kiku dake de, <u>ochitsuku</u>.
あなたの**声**を聞くだけで、<u>落ち着く</u>。
Just hearing your **voice** <u>calms</u> me down.

This expresses that one simple action is enough to cause the result.
For better comprehension, here is a side-by-side comparison:

Form	Meaning	Example
X + だけ	only / just	Pan dake tabeta パンだけ食べた (I only ate bread)
Verb-dictionary + だけ	as much as / as far as / to your heart's content	Suki na dake totte ii yo 好きなだけ取っていいよ (Take as much as you like)
X + だけで	just by / simply by	Kiku dake de, ochitsuku 聞くだけで落ち着く (Just hearing it calms me)

Later in the book, you'll learn another pattern that also means "only": しか～ない. Unlike だけ, which is neutral and works with any verb, しか always appears together with a negative verb (～ない) and carries a stronger "nothing but X" nuance. We'll cover しか～ない in Part V.

Koso こそ :

This emphatic particle adds strong emphasis to the word it follows: "this and no other," "exactly this," "precisely this." こそ highlights the speaker's focus. Think of it as putting a verbal spotlight on a word.

1) Emphasis on the subject or topic ("THIS is the one").

Kyou koso, <u>ganbarou</u> to omou.
今日こそ、<u>がんばろう</u>と思う。
Today is the day I'm determined to <u>do my best</u>.
Here, こそ emphasizes today — not yesterday, not tomorrow.

Note: to omou (と + 思う) has two major functions.
A) "I think that…"
Used for opinions, guesses, beliefs.

- **Ashita** wa ame da to omou.
  明日は雨だと思う。
  I think it will rain **tomorrow**.

B) "I intend to…" / "I'm planning to…"
Used when the clause before と is a volitional form (～よう / ～おう).

- Nihon ni ikou to omou.
  日本に行こうと思う。
  I'm thinking of going to Japan.

(Meaning: I intend to / I'm planning to / I'm determined to.)

The pattern ～おうと思う expresses intention or resolve ("I intend to…/I'm determined to…") The determination comes from the volitional form (～おう), not from 思う itself.

Why (Kyou koso, ganbarou to omou) can't mean "I think I will do my best": Because Japanese does not use 思う for "I think I will ___" in the English sense of "I guess I'll ___."
English:
"I think I'll go now." (soft decision)
Japanese:
Sorosoro kaerou ka na / そろそろ帰ろうかな。
(Not "Kaerou to omou" "帰ろうと思う" unless you mean "I've decided to go home.")

2) Emphasis in expressions of gratitude or reciprocity.
こそ often appears in polite exchanges to emphasize "No, it is I who…"

Kochira koso, arigatou gozaimasu.
こちらこそ、ありがとうございます。
No, thank you (It is I who should be thanking you).
Here, こそ emphasizes こちら ("I / we"), flipping the gratitude back.

Note: こちら literally means "this side," but in polite Japanese it also means "I / we." In こちらこそ, it means "No, I (on this side) am the one who should say that." English drops the spatial meaning and translates it as "No, thank you."

3) Emphasis in contrast ("THIS is what matters").
こそ can highlight the true or important point.

Mondai koso, sono **taido** da.
問題こそ、その態度だ。
The real problem is your **attitude**.
Here, こそ marks 問題 (the problem) as the true focus.

For better comprehension, here is a side-by-side comparison:

Form	Meaning	Example
X + こそ	exactly / precisely / this and no other	Kyō koso ganbarou to omou / 今日こそ頑張ろうと思う (Today is the day I'll do my best)
こちらこそ	polite reciprocity ("No, I should say…")	Kochira koso arigatō こちらこそありがとう (No, thank you)
X はこそ	strong contrast ("THIS is the real…")	Mondai koso taido da 問題こそ態度だ (The real issue is the attitude)

Nante なんて:

Depending on tone and context, なんて expresses the speaker's emotional reaction to a noun, phrase, or entire clause. It can convey:

- Surprise: "Wow, that happened?" / "I can't believe…"
  Kare ga kuru nante, **hontō** ni bikkuri shita.
  彼が来るなんて、本当にびっくりした。
  That he would come—I was **really** surprised.

- Disbelief or disappointment: "I can't believe this…"
  Anna koto o iu nante, shinjirarenai
  あんなことを言うなんて、信じられない
  I can't believe he'd say something **like that**
  - konna こんな = like this (near me)
  - sonna そんな = like that (near you)
  - anna あんな = like that (far from both of us)

- Admiration: "How wonderful that…"
  Konna ni utsukushii keshiki ga mirareru nante, **shiawase** da.
  こんなに美しい景色が見られるなんて、**幸せ**だ。

To be able to see such a beautiful view—I feel so **lucky**.

- Dismissiveness: "Something like that… (ugh!)"
  Anna eiga nante, miru ki **mo** shinai.
  あんな映画なんて、見る気もしない。
  A movie like that? I don't **even** feel like watching it.

In English, we often name the emotion directly ("I was surprised that he came"). In Japanese, the emotion is embedded in the structure:

Kare ga kuru nante!
彼が来るなんて！
That he would come—! (surprise, disbelief, or admiration depending on tone)

> Note: なんて is not a vocabulary word meaning "surprised" or "disbelief." It is an emotional marker. Japanese has explicit words for those emotions (e.g., odoroita 驚いた "was surprised," fushin 不信 "disbelief"), but なんて expresses the reaction indirectly and more naturally.

Sa (さ):

Sentence-ending particle / interjectory particle that adds casualness, softness, or emotional coloring to a statement. It can make speech sound: relaxed, confident, offhand, slightly emphatic, or imply "you know…" / "come on…" / "well…" It does not change the grammatical meaning, but it changes the tone. It can appear at the beginning, middle, or end of a sentence, and its meaning depends on tone rather than grammar.

1. Sentence-ending さ — casual softener / emotional color. Used at the end of a sentence to add a relaxed, friendly, or lightly emphatic tone. Often feels like "you know," "yeah," "come on," or "that's just how it is."

Mā, sō sa.
まあ、そうさ。
Well, that's how it is, you know.

Nuance: Without さ → neutral: "Well, that's how it is."
With さ → softer, more conversational, slightly shrugging.

> Note: まあ (maa) is a soft, shrug-like filler meaning "well…" or "I guess…," used to ease into a statement with a gentle, non-committal tone. It is covered in depth in Part VIII: OTHER IMPORTANT WORDS.

2. Mid-sentence さ — filler / casual emphasis. Inserted inside a sentence to keep the tone light, casual, or slightly assertive. Often used by men, but not exclusively.

A) 昨日さ、図書館に行ったらさ、ケンジくんがいたよ。
Kino sa, toshokan ni ittara sa, Kenji-kun ga ita yo.
"So **yesterday**, I went to the library, you know? And Kenji was there!"
Here it's like English "man," "like," "you know," or a casual beat in the rhythm.

Note: 行ったら (ittara) is the conditional form of 行く (iku):

- 行く → 行った → 行ったら
- iku → itta → ittara
- "go" → "went" → "if/when (someone) goes/went"

So:

- 行った (itta) = went
- 行ったら (ittara) = if/when (someone) goes / if/when (someone) went

The ら at the end is the giveaway: it marks a conditional ("if/when").

B) **Sonna** koto sa, ki ni suru na yo.
そんなことさ、気にするなよ。
That kind of thing, you know, don't worry about it.

Nuance: Adds a breezy, informal rhythm — like tossing in "man," "you know," or "hey."

Breakdown of 気にする (ki ni suru):
気 (ki) = mind, mood, feelings, attention, concern
に (ni) = target marker ("toward," "about")
する (suru) = to do

Put together:
気にする = "to put your mind on something," "to worry about something," "to be bothered by something."

Now add the negative command:
するな = "don't do (it)" (plain negative command)
よ = softening/emphasis particle ("you know," "okay," "I'm telling you")

So: 気にするなよ

= "Don't put your mind on it, okay?"
= "Don't let it bother you."
= "Don't worry about it."
This is the natural English equivalent. English doesn't have a direct expression for "put your mind on X," so "Don't worry about it" is the closest natural translation.

3. さ as a "reset" or "lead-in" word (interjection). Used at the start of a sentence to shift gears, gather thoughts, or introduce a point. Similar to "So…," "Well…," or "Alright…"

Sa, ikō ka.
さ、行こうか。
Alright, let's go.

Nuance: Light, friendly, often used when transitioning to action.

Note: In the above example, か is not the normal question-marking か. It's a sentence-ending softener that turns the invitation into a gentle suggestion, not a question.

1) The question-marking か:
This is the one beginners learn first:
- 行きますか。

"Are you going?"
Here, か marks a real question and expects an answer.

2) The invitation / suggestion か:
In 行こうか, か attaches to the volitional form (行こう), and the meaning changes completely:
- 行こう = "Let's go."
- 行こうか = "Shall we go?" / "Let's go, okay?"

This か does not mark a question in the information-seeking sense.
It softens the volitional and makes it:
- less forceful
- more collaborative
- more "checking in" with the listener

It's closer to English "shall we…?" or "let's…, yeah?"

3) Why learners get confused:
Because the surface form is the same か, but the grammar underneath is different:

- After plain form → か = question marker
- After volitional form → か = suggestion softener

So in:
さ、行こうか。
Sa, ikō ka.
The か is not asking "Are we going?" It's softening "Let's go."

4. さ for mild insistence / confidence. Adds a tone of casual certainty, not aggressive, but confident and relaxed.

Daijōbu sa.
大丈夫さ。
It's **fine**, really.

Nuance: feels reassuring, almost like a gentle pat on the shoulder.

Tte って:

The Casual "Speaking / Pointing / Quoting" Particle. って is a very common, informal particle used in spoken Japanese. Think of it as a soft, flexible tool that does three things in casual speech:
• It marks what you're talking about (topic marker, like a casual は).
• It quotes what someone said or thought (like "that…" or "you know…").
• It adds emphasis or highlights the word before it.
It's informal, friendly, and extremely common in everyday speech.

1) って as a casual TOPIC marker. It is used when introducing or highlighting a topic in a relaxed way.

Ashita tte ame?
明日って雨?
About **tomorrow** — is it going to rain?

Kanojo tte yasashii yo ne.
彼女って優しいよね。
She's really kind, you know.

Here, the nuance is pointing at a topic, drawing attention, adds mild emphasis, and provides a casual, spoken tone.

Note: ね (ne) is a sentence-ending particle used when the speaker seeks agreement, confirmation, or shared understanding. It softens the tone and invites the listener to align with the speaker's feeling.
よ (yo), on the other hand, adds emphasis. It asserts the speaker's stance or highlights information the speaker wants the listener to notice. When used before ね, it reinforces the statement while still inviting agreement.
Together, よね (yo ne) combines both effects: a gentle assertion followed by a request for shared understanding. It's explained in full detail in Part II: Questions & Uncertainty.

2) って as a QUOTING particle ("that…", "I heard…", "you said…"). This is the most common use.

"Iku" tte **itta** yo ne.
「行く」って**言っ**たよね。
You **said** "I'm going," right?

Note: Japanese often omits pronouns like "you" when the meaning is already clear from context. Using anata or naming the person directly can feel overly pointed, too direct, or even confrontational in everyday conversation. In this sentence, the listener already knows who is being addressed, so Japanese simply states:

- 「行く」って言ったよね。

Said "I'm going," right?
The subject "you" is understood without being spoken.

Kare, **konai** tte.
彼、**来ない**って。
He said he's **not coming**. / I heard he's **not coming**.

Here, the nuance is quoting speech or thoughts, reporting information, adds a casual and conversational tone.

3) って for SELF-QUOTING (internal thoughts).

Dō shiyō kana tte omotta.
どうしようかなって思った。
I was thinking, "What should I do…?"

Here, the nuance is quoting your own thoughts, makes it soft, reflective, and blends perfectly with かな, which is covered in detail in Part II: Agreement & Reflection. In brief, かな is a soft internal wondering often used when thinking to oneself. It adds uncertainty, hesitation, or quiet contemplation. Sort of like saying: Hmm, I wonder…

Note: って also appears inside common conversational expressions like (tte iu ka) っていうか ("I mean…" / "Or rather…") and (tte kanji) って感じ ("kind of like…"). These are simply built from the same quoting って.
Examples:
1. っていうか — "I mean… / or rather… / more like…"

Kono **fuku**, kawaii… tte iu ka, chotto mezurashii ne.
この服、かわいい…っていうか、ちょっと珍しいね。
This **outfit** is cute… I mean, it's kind of unusual.

2. って感じ — "kind of like… / feels like… / sort of…" Used to describe an impression, a "feel," not a precise fact.

Kore wa **haru** tte kanji.
これは春って感じ。
This feels like **spring**.

Yo よ:

A sentence-ending particle that adds assertion, emphasis, or new information from the speaker to the listener. It signals: "I'm telling you this," "I want you to know," "I'm asserting this point." よ does not change the factual meaning of a sentence — it changes the speaker's stance toward the listener.

1) Strong assertion / confident statement. Used when the speaker asserts something clearly and confidently.

Ashita wa **yasumi** da yo.
明日は休みだよ。
Tomorrow is a **day off**, you know.

Meaning: asserting information the listener may not know.

2) Casual emphasis (neutral tone). Used to add friendly emphasis or soften a statement while still asserting it.

Kore, sugoku oishii yo.
これ、すごくおいしいよ。
This is really good.

Meaning: casual, friendly emphasis.

3) Masculine tone (rougher, stronger よ). In masculine speech, よ can sound firmer, more direct, or more "punchy." Often paired with ぞ or な for even stronger effect.

Ore ga yaru yo.
俺がやるよ。
I'll do it.

Meaning: confident, slightly forceful assertion. This is not "male-only," but it leans masculine in tone.

> Side-Note: 俺 (ore) is a first-person pronoun. It is a casual, masculine way to say "I." It's commonly used by men among friends, in relaxed settings, or in fiction to give a character a strong, confident, or rough tone.
> It is not rude, but it is not polite. Beginners should avoid using it in formal situations.
>
> Tone summary
> - watashi = neutral → polite
> - boku = soft, boyish, gentle
> - ore = strong, casual, masculine

4) Soft, feminine, or gentle よ. When spoken softly, よ can sound warm, reassuring, or gentle.

Mada **jikan** aru yo.
まだ**時間**あるよ。
There's still **time**.
Meaning: comforting reassurance. Tone, not grammar, creates the "feminine" feel.

5) よ used to correct or clarify. Used when the speaker provides correct information or contradicts a mistaken assumption.

Soko ja nai yo.
そこじゃないよ。
Not there.
Meaning: correcting the listener gently but clearly.

6) よ with commands (softens or encourages). よ can make a command sound more encouraging and less harsh.

Hayaku kite yo.
早く来てよ。
Come **quickly**, okay?
Meaning: urging, but not barking an order.

7) よ with invitations (friendly, warm). Adds friendliness or enthusiasm.

Issho ni ikou yo.
一緒に行こうよ。
Let's go **together**!
Meaning: warm, inviting emphasis.

8) よね vs よ. よね combines assertion (よ) + seeking agreement (ね).

Kore, kirei da yo ne.
これ、きれいだよね。
This is pretty, isn't it?
Meaning: asserting while inviting the listener to agree. よ alone = "I'm telling you."
よね = "I'm telling you, and you agree, right?"

9) よ in masculine rough speech: よぞ / よな. These are advanced but common in fiction and casual male dialogue.

Kyou wa **makenai** yo zo.
今日は**負けない**よぞ。
I'm **not losing** today!
Meaning: strong, almost theatrical assertion.

Ii **tenki** da yo na.
いい**天気**だよな。
Nice **weather**, huh.
Meaning: masculine, reflective, slightly rough.

10) よ in feminine soft speech: yo～ / よ～ (intonation). It is not grammar, but intonation. A long, rising よ can sound cute, soft, or playful.

Mou, ikuyo～
もう、行くよ～
Come on, I'm going!
Meaning: soft, playful emphasis.

よ adds the speaker's stance: "I'm telling you this." Depending on tone, it can sound assertive, friendly, masculine, gentle, corrective, or encouraging.

Ze ぜ:

A sentence-ending particle that adds strong, rough, masculine emphasis. It signals confidence, boldness, enthusiasm, or a slightly tough attitude. It is casual, informal, and almost always used by men (especially in fiction, anime, and casual male speech). ぜ does not change the factual meaning, it changes the speaker's energy.

1) Strong, masculine assertion. Used when the speaker asserts something boldly or confidently.

Ore wa iku ze.
俺は行くぜ。
I'm going.
Meaning: confident, masculine emphasis.

2) Pumping oneself up / expressing determination. ぜ often appears when the speaker is psyching themselves up or declaring resolve.

Kyou wa **katsu** ze!
今日は**勝つ**ぜ！
I'm **winning** today!
Meaning: self-motivation with a strong, energetic tone.

3) Friendly, rough enthusiasm. ぜ can sound upbeat and energetic among male friends.

Yatta ze!
やったぜ！
We did it! / Yeah!
Meaning: celebratory, rough excitement.

4) Rough encouragement or urging. ぜ can be used to push someone forward in a friendly but forceful way.

Issho ni yarou ze.
一緒にやろうぜ。
Let's do it **together**.
Meaning: urging with a masculine, energetic vibe.

5) Rough warning or reminder. ぜ can add a tough edge to a warning.

<u>Osoi</u> to **okureru** ze.
<u>遅い</u>と**遅れる**ぜ。
If you're <u>slow</u>, you'll **miss** it.
Meaning: rough, cautionary tone.

6) ぜ after ぞ (ぜぞ) — very rough, theatrical. Rare in real life but common in manga/anime for dramatic effect.

Kakugo shiro ze zo!
覚悟しろぜぞ！
Prepare yourself!
Meaning: exaggerated, stylized roughness.

> Note: Kakugo (覚悟) is "mental readiness," "resolve," "preparedness for what's coming." 覚悟 is not the act of preparing (that would be 準備する (junbi suru)).
> 覚悟 is the inner decision to face something difficult, dangerous, painful, or unavoidable.

Zo ぞ:

A sentence-ending particle that adds strong, rough, masculine force to a statement. It signals: "Listen up," "This is serious," "I'm declaring this," or "I mean it." ぞ is casual, informal, and strongly associated with masculine or tough speech. It does not change the factual meaning — it changes the speaker's intensity.

1) Strong, forceful assertion. Used when the speaker declares something with power or conviction.

Ore wa iku zo.
俺は行くぞ。
I'm going.
Meaning: strong, forceful declaration.

2) Warning or threat (rough, serious tone). ぞ adds a sharp edge when the speaker warns someone.

<u>Yoku</u> **kiite** oku zo.
<u>よく</u>**聞い**ておくぞ。
I'm going to **listen** <u>carefully</u> (and keep it in my mind)!

Meaning: declaring their intent to listen carefully.

> Side-Note: 〜ておく (te-oku) is a helper-verb pattern that means to do something in advance or to prepare by doing something now. It adds the idea of "do this now so you're ready later." In **聞いておく**, the meaning becomes: "listen now and keep it in mind," "listen carefully so you're prepared."
>
> This is why よく聞いておくぞ feels like a serious instruction or warning. Note: 〜ておく will be explained in full detail in Part IV: Explanatory & Causal.

Yamero yo… tte **itta** zo.
やめろよ…って**言った**ぞ。
I **told you** to stop.
Meaning: rough warning.

> Side-Note: って (tte) can act as a soft topic marker or highlighter in casual speech. In this sentence, however, って is the quoting form ("…that…"). We covered both uses earlier in this section, and it appears here again as a refresher because it's extremely common in casual Japanese.
>
> Side-Note: itta (言った) in this sentence means "said", but the natural English translation becomes "told you" because of how Japanese handles quoting.

3) Pumping oneself up / determination (stronger than ぜ). ぞ expresses a more serious, battle-ready determination.

Kyou wa **makenai** zo!
今日は**負けない**ぞ！
I'm **not losing** today!
Meaning: strong, determined resolve. (Compare with ぜ, which feels more upbeat and energetic.)

4) Calling attention / emphasizing importance. ぞ can function like a verbal spotlight: "Pay attention to this."

Kore wa **taisetsu** da zo.
これは**大切**だぞ。
This is **important**.
Meaning: emphasizing significance with force.

5) Rough encouragement (stronger push than ぜ). Used to push someone forward with a tough, commanding vibe.

Ganbaru zo!
頑張るぞ！
Let's do this! / I'll **give it my all**!

Meaning: strong, rallying energy.

6) Rough, dramatic tone in fiction. ぞ is extremely common in manga, anime, and games to signal a character's toughness, confidence, or intensity.

Kakugo suru n da zo!
覚悟するんだぞ！
You'd better **be ready**!

Meaning: strong, dramatic warning.

7) ぞ in softer or older-male speech. In some contexts, especially with older men, ぞ can sound less aggressive and more like a firm, matter-of-fact emphasis.

Mō **kaeru** zo.
もう帰るぞ。
I'm **heading home** now.

Meaning: firm, not necessarily angry. Tone depends heavily on voice and context.

ぜ vs よ vs ぞ (quick comparison)

Particle	Tone	Meaning
よ	neutral → friendly	"I'm telling you."
ぞ	strong, rough	"Listen up!" / "This is serious."
ぜ	strong but upbeat	"Let's go!" / "I'm fired up!"

PART II: AGREEMENT & REFLECTION

Key stems and nuances in this section:

- iin いいん → Contraction of ii no da, reflective assertion
- kana かな → Reflective wondering, softer than kashira かしら
- ndesu んです → Explanatory softening, polite nuance
- na な, naa なあ, ne ね, wa わ, yo ne よね → Seeking agreement, softening, reflection, feminine tone.

Vocabulary to review:

anzen	安全	safety
betsu	別	separate, different, another, distinct
haru	春	spring
isogashii	忙しい	busy / mentally preoccupied or restless
itai	痛い	it hurts, painful
kanashii	悲しい	sad
keshiki	景色	view, scenery
komaru	困る	to be troubled / to be in difficulty
kuyashii	悔しい	frustrating, regrettable
mayou	迷う	to be unsure / to hesitate / to be lost (physically or mentally)
mondai	問題	problem, issue
naru	なる	to become
natsukashī	懐かしい	nostalgic, memories
shizuka	静か	quiet
taihen	大変	tough / hard
teinei	丁寧	polite, careful
tokui	得意	skillfull, good at
mukashi	昔	long ago
ureshii	嬉しい	happy, glad
yūmei	有名	famous
yukkuri	ゆっくり	slowly / take your time / calmly

Diving further into the stems and nuances

Iin いいん:

A contraction of いい + のです ("it's good / it's fine / it's okay, you see"). It must be followed by です or だ:

- いいんです (polite)
- いいんだ (casual)

The ん adds an explanatory or softening nuance, making the phrase feel like "It's fine because…" or "It's okay, really."

1. いいんです (polite, explanatory, gentle)

A. Giving reassurance:
Sore de ī ndesu
それでいいんです
That's fine, really
→ nuance: "Don't worry, that's acceptable."

B. Explaining a reason:
Kyō wa ikanakute ī ndesu
今日は行かなくていいんです
It's okay if I don't go today, you see
→ nuance: "There's a reason I don't have to go."

C. Soft refusal:
Ima wa ī ndesu.
今はいいんです。
I'm okay for now, thanks.
→ nuance: "I'm declining, but gently."

2. いいんだ (casual, warm, emotional)

A. Reassuring a friend:
Sore de ī nda yo.
それでいいんだよ。
That's totally fine.
→ nuance: comforting, supportive.

B. Explaining your own decision:
Kore de ī nda.
これでいいんだ。
This is fine (for my reasons).
→ nuance: "I've thought about it, and this is okay."

C. Softly correcting someone:
Betsu ni ki ni shinakute ī nda.
別に気にしなくていいんだ。
You really don't need to worry about it.
→ nuance: gentle, friendly reassurance.

Betsu (別) by itself means: separate, different, another, distinct.
Examples:
Betsu no hito.
別の人。
A different person.

Betsu no mondai.
別の問題。
A separate issue.

Betsu ni takes the core meaning of 別 ("separate / nothing in particular") and turns it into an adverb meaning "not particularly" when used with a negative verb.

Betsu ni (別に) as a phrase. When followed by a negative verb, it means: not particularly, not really, it's nothing special, I don't especially…
Example:
Betsu ni ki ni shite nai.
別に気にしてない。
I'm not really worried about it.

Why there are two に in "別に気にしてない":
Even though they look the same, the two に have completely different functions. Let's break it down:
1) 別に (betsu ni) — adverb meaning "not particularly / not really"

- 別 (betsu) = separate, different, nothing special
- に (ni) = turns 別 into an adverb

So 別に becomes: "not particularly / not really / nothing in particular."

This に is part of a fixed expression that almost always appears with a negative verb.

2) 気に (ki ni) — part of the phrase 気にする ("to care / to

worry / to mind”). Here, に is a case particle marking what the person “puts their feelings/attention on.”

- 気 (ki) = mind, feelings
- に (ni) = particle meaning “toward / about”
- する = to do

So 気にする literally means: “to do toward the mind” → “to care / to worry about.”

In the negative:

- 気にしない = don’t worry about it
- 気にしてない = not worrying about it (casual)

This に is a grammatical particle, not part of a set phrase. The “separate / nothing special” idea of 別 becomes: There’s nothing in particular (to worry about).

3. Contrast with plain いいです (no explanation, no emotional shading)

Plain:
それでいいです。
That’s fine.
→ neutral, factual, no warmth.

Explanatory:
それでいいんです。
That’s fine, you see.
→ soft, reassuring, gives emotional context.

Kana かな:

A sentence-ending particle used to express contemplation, uncertainty, or mild hope. It’s often used when thinking aloud, wondering about something, or expressing a tentative opinion. It’s not a direct question like か, but more of a soft musing.

JAPANESE	TRANSLATION	NUANCE
Dō shiyou kana どうしようかな	What should I do, I wonder	Thinking aloud, unsure
Ashita, ame kana 明日、雨かな	I wonder if it’ll rain tomorrow	Mild speculation
Kare, kuru kana? 彼、来るかな？	I wonder if he’ll come	Uncertain, casual musing
Dekiru kana… できるかな…	I wonder if I can do it…	Self-doubt or hope

かな is used more in casual speech, especially by men (though women use it too). In polite speech, you might hear "deshou ka" でしょうか or "kamo shiremasen" かもしれません instead. It's often accompanied by a trailing tone or ellipsis in writing, reflecting its introspective feel.

Note: When you add って (tte) to かな, you get: kanatte かなって. Which roughly means: "I was thinking…", "I was wondering…", or "I was like, maybe…" It's a casual, reflective phrase that turns the internal musing of かな into a quoted or remembered thought — often used when recounting what you (or someone else) was thinking.
かなって is not a new grammar point — it's simply かな + the informal quotation particle って (covered in Part 1: Assertion & Emphasis).

JAPANESE	TRANSLATION	NUANCE
Ikou kanatte omotteta 行こうかなって思ってた	I was thinking maybe I'd go	Reflective, casual
Kare, kuru kanatte… 彼、来るかなって…	I was wondering if he'd come…	Soft, trailing thought
Kore de ī no kanatte omou toki ga aru. これでいいのかなって思う時がある	There are times I wonder if this is really **okay**	Ongoing self-doubt

かな after nouns sometimes appears as かなあ (with an extra "a" sound). This is especially common when expressing: longing, mild hope, wistfulness. It's the same meaning, just more emotional / drawn-out. Similar to how English speakers might write "so" vs. "sooo," it shifts the tone from a simple "I wonder…" to a more drawn-out "I really wonder…"

Example:

- Natsuyasumi, hayaku konai kanā.
  夏休み、早く来ないかなあ。
  I wish summer break would come soon…

Kashira かしら:

A sentence-ending particle expressing soft, reflective wondering. It's introspective and gentle, often used when thinking aloud.

- Traditionally feminine, especially in modern standard Japanese
- Still used by women of all ages
- Rare for men in contemporary speech (except in stylized, humorous, or character-voice contexts)
- Parallels かな, but with a softer, more delicate emotional feel

Kyō, kare wa **kuru** kashira.
今日、彼は**来る**かしら。
I wonder if he'll **come** today.

Nuance: soft, feminine-leaning musing; thinking aloud rather than asking for an answer.

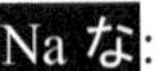:

Functions as a sentence-ending particle or a na-adjective marker. As a sentence-ending particle, it adds emotional coloring — often soft reflection, emphasis, or talking to oneself. It's not the same as the na-adjective marker (like in kirei na hana - きれい な 花 - beautiful flowers). This is a final particle. When you say なつかしいな, you're not just stating "this is nostalgic." You're sighing it out, almost like:

- "Ah, this is **nostalgic**…" "**Natsukashī** na." "**懐かしい**な。"
- "Wow, that brings back memories."
- "How nostalgic this feels."

It's often used when you're speaking to yourself or expressing a feeling aloud, rather than directly addressing someone.

Let's back up a bit. As a na-adjective marker, you'll need to understand the difference between an i-adjective and a na-adjective.

i-adjectives

- Almost always end with い (i) in their dictionary form. When a word ends in -shi (し), the final sound is shi, and is not considered as the vowel i. To be considered an i-adjective, it must have the extra い (i) at the end of an adjective ending with shi (し). This is exactly the kind of subtlety that trips up beginners.

Examples:

- 暑い (atsui) = hot
- 高い (takai) = tall, expensive
- 面白い (omoshiroi) = interesting
- 嬉しい (ureshii) = happy, glad
- 悲しい (kanashii) = sad
- 悔しい (kuyashii) = frustrating, regrettable

If it ends in い, it's usually an i-adjective.

na-adjectives

- Do not end with い (most of the time – see below.)
  [Remember, shi (し) is not the vowel i (い)]
- When they describe a noun, they need な before it.

Example:

- 大切な友達 (taisetsu na tomodachi) = an important friend
- 静かな町 (shizuka na machi) = a quiet town
- 安全な場所 (anzen na basho) = a safe place

Note: There are some words that end with i (い) that are still considered a na-adjective. This is one of those "gotcha" moments in Japanese grammar that every learner bumps into. Let's break it down clearly.

Take for example きれい (kirei). At first glance, きれい ends with い, so it looks like an i-adjective. But historically, きれい is not a native Japanese adjective. It comes from classical Chinese compounds (via Sino-Japanese vocabulary). Many Sino-Japanese words end in -ei (えい), which just happens to end with the kana い. That final い is part of the えい (ei) sound, not the adjective marker い that defines i-adjectives.

These are not extremely numerous. They form a small, memorable set compared to the hundreds of true i-adjectives. Most textbooks and reference guides do list them explicitly, often in a special section called "Na-adjectives ending in -i". Once you memorize this handful, the rest of the na-adjectives are easy to recognize because they don't end in い at all.

Here are a few more "tricky na-adjectives ending in い:

kirai	嫌い	dislike, hate
teinei	丁寧	polite, careful
tokui	得意	skillfull, good at
yūmei	有名	famous

Naa なあ:

A sentence-ending particle expressing stronger, deeper, or more drawn-out emotion than な. It can show: wistful reflection, admiration, longing, mild complaint, emotional emphasis, talking to oneself with feeling.

The long vowel ああ signals that the emotion is drawn out — like a sigh, a murmur, or a moment of feeling. It is not gendered. Both men and women use it naturally. The primary uses of なあ are:

1) Reflective emotion (nostalgia, longing, quiet feeling). Used when the speaker is thinking aloud with emotion.

Mukashi no shashin o miru to, natsukashī nā.
昔の写真を見ると、なつかしいなあ。
When I look at **old** photos, it really feels nostalgic…
Nuance: deeper, more heartfelt than な.

2) Admiration or being impressed. It expresses a soft exclamation of "wow," "that's amazing," "beautiful," etc.

Kono **keshiki**, kirei da nā.
この**景色**、きれいだなあ。
This **view** is so beautiful…
Nuance: admiration mixed with personal feeling.

> Side-note: だ (da) is the plain form of the polite です (desu). It attaches to nouns and na-adjectives to express "is / am / are."

3) It expresses mild complaint or emotional frustration; not angry, just expressing a feeling aloud.

Mata densha ga **okure** teru nā.
また電車が**遅れ**てるなあ。
Ugh, the train's **late** again…
Nuance: gentle frustration, not directed at anyone.

> Side-note: てる is the casual spoken contraction of ている, the helper-verb construction that expresses progressive, habitual, or resulting state. In the example above, okure te iru → okure teru. This contraction is covered fully in Section VIII.

4) It expresses wishing or hoping (internal, not directed at someone). A quiet "I wish…" or "I hope…"

Hayaku **haru** ni naranai ka nā.
早く**春**にならないかなあ。
I wish **spring** would come soon…

Nuance: longing, soft desire.

IMPORTANT: At first glance, ならない (naranai) is the negative form of なる ("to become"). So why doesn't it mean: "I don't want it to become spring" or "It won't become spring"? Because in this construction, the negative is not literal. It's part of a soft, emotional pattern used to express longing or wishing. Even though ならない is grammatically negative, the emotional meaning of the whole pattern is positive.

The real structure: 〜ないかなあ (nai ka naa) = "I wonder if it would…" / "I wish it would…" This pattern: V-ない + かなあ does not express negation. It expresses: hope, longing, a gentle wish, "I wonder if it might…", "I wish it would…"

It's similar to English expressions like: "Wouldn't it be nice if…?", "I wonder if it might…", "I wish it would…"
These also use negative forms but don't feel negative.

Japanese often uses negative forms to express: soft requests, indirect hopes, gentle suggestions, polite hesitation because the negative form feels less forceful, it becomes a natural way to express: "I wish X would happen, but I know I can't control it."

N-desu / no desu んです / のです:

A sentence-ending explanatory construction that adds background, emotion, clarification, or softening. It answers the unspoken question: "Why?" / "What's the reason?" / "What's the situation?" It does not change the basic meaning of the sentence — it adds nuance.

N-desu (んです) and no desu (のです) are the same construction. The meaning, function, and nuance are identical. The only difference is formality and style:

Form	Usage	Tone
んです	everyday speech	natural, conversational
のです	formal writing, careful speech	slightly more literary or explanatory

Why they're the same: ん is simply the phonetic contraction of の:

- のです (no desu) → んです (ndesu)
- のだ (no da) → んだ (nda)

Nothing changes in meaning. It's like English "I am" → "I'm."

1) Giving an explanation (the core meaning). Used when the speaker provides background or a reason.

Atama ga itai n desu.
頭が痛いんです。
My **head** hurts (that's why).

Nuance: You're not just stating a fact, you're explaining the situation.

Dōshite **konakatta** n desu ka.
どうして**来なかった**んですか。
Why **didn't you come** (what happened)?

Nuance: The んです signals you want the reason, not just the fact.

2) Softening a statement (making it less blunt). Plain statements can sound abrupt. Adding んです makes them gentle and polite.

Chotto **isogashii** n desu.
ちょっと**忙しい**んです。
I'm a bit **busy** (sorry).

Nuance: Softer than 忙しいです, which can feel curt.

3) Emphasizing a situation or feeling. Adds emotional weight, surprise, frustration, insistence, or personal feeling.

Hontō ni ikitai n desu.
本当に行きたいんです。
I **really** want to go.

Nuance: heartfelt emphasis.

Komatte iru n desu.
困っているんです。
I'm having **trouble**, you see.

Nuance: asking for understanding.

4) Asking for explanation or clarification. When used in questions, it signals curiosity, concern, or desire for background.

Nani o shite iru n desu ka.
何をしているんですか。
What are you doing (what's going on)?
Here, it asks for context. Not just "What are you doing?"

Dō shita n desu ka.
どうしたんですか。
What happened (are you okay)?
Nuance: emotional concern.

5) Introducing a reason before a request or suggestion. A classic pattern in polite Japanese: Reason + んですが… + request/suggestion.

Michi ni mayotte iru n desu ga, **eki** wa doko desu ka.
道に迷っているんですが、**駅**はどこですか。
I'm lost, so… where is the **station**?

Nuance: The んですが softens the request by giving context first.

> Note: Mayotte (迷って) does NOT mean "lost" by itself. It means "to be confused / to be uncertain / to hesitate / to be lost (mentally or directionally)" depending on context. Because it's broad, Japanese often adds 道 (michi) to clarify what kind of "lost" you mean. (In English, we don't say "I'm street lost.")

んです works with all stems:

- Verb stems: taberu ndesu 食べるんです, iku ndesu 行くんです
- Adjective stems: samui ndesu 寒いんです, shizukana ndesu 静かなんです
- Noun stems: gakuseina ndesu 学生なんです

な appears before んです for nouns and na-adjectives

- Shizukana ndesu 静かなんです (It's quiet)
- Gakuseina ndesu 学生なんです (I'm a student)

んです does not add new information. It adds the speaker's stance toward the information (explanation, emotion, or softening).

Ne ね:

A sentence-ending particle that seeks agreement, shared feeling, or confirmation. It softens statements, invites connection, and checks whether the listener shares the same understanding. Its core meaning is: "Right?" / "Isn't it?" / "You know?" / "Don't you think?" But the nuance shifts depending on tone and context.

1) Seeking agreement (the core meaning). Used when the speaker expects the listener to agree.

Kyō wa **samui** ne.
今日は**寒い**ね。
It's **cold** today, isn't it?

Nuance: You're inviting the listener to share the feeling.

2) Softening a statement (making it friendly or gentle). ね can make a statement less blunt or more warm.

Yukkuri de ii desu yo ne.
ゆっくりでいいですよね。
Take your time, okay?

Nuance: Friendly reassurance, not a command.

> Note: Yukkuri de ii desu yo ne (ゆっくりでいいですよね) can mean either "It's okay to take your time, right?" or "Take your time, okay?" depending on whether you emphasize the confirmation (ね) or the reassurance (ですよ). Both capture the same gentle, unhurried tone.

3) Confirming information (checking understanding). Used when the speaker wants to verify something they believe is true.

Ashita, kuru n da yo ne.
明日、来るんだよね。
You're coming **tomorrow**, right?
Nuance: You think it's true, but you want confirmation.

4) Expressing shared emotion (bonding, empathy). ね can show sympathy, surprise, or shared feeling.

Taihen datta ne.
大変だったね。
That must have been **tough**.
Nuance: Emotional connection.

5) Softening a request (making it polite and less direct). Adding ね makes a request sound more cooperative.

Chotto **matte** ne.
ちょっと**待って**ね。
Wait a moment, okay?
Nuance: Gentle, friendly request.

6) Expressing admiration or surprise. Tone of voice matters here, rising intonation adds emotion.

Kirei da ne!
きれいだね！
It's **beautiful**!
Nuance: Warm admiration.

7) Filling silence / keeping the conversation flowing. In casual speech, ね can act like a soft conversational cushion.

Sō da ne…
そうだね…
"Yeah…" / "I see…"
Nuance: Thinking, agreeing, or keeping the rhythm.

Wa わ:

It's a sentence-ending particle, not a grammatical marker like は. It has two major uses, depending on region and gender.

1) わ as a sentence-ending particle (feminine / gentle). This is the most well-known わ and it is used mainly by women (especially in older or traditional speech) to add: softness, light emphasis, emotional coloring, gentle assertion. It does not seek agreement like ね. It's more like a soft, feminine よ.

Kirei da wa.
きれいだわ。
"It's beautiful."

Kyō wa isogashii wa.
今日は忙しいわ。
"I'm busy **today**."

Hontō ni sō omou wa.
本当にそう思うわ。
"I **really** think so."

2) わ in Kansai dialect (gender-neutral, stronger). In Kansai (Osaka, Kyoto, etc.), わ is used by men and women and has a stronger, more assertive feel. It's closer to よ or ぞ in tone. Examples:

Iku wa!
行くわ！
"I'm **going**!"

Shiran wa!
知らんわ！
"I **don't know**!"
This is not feminine, it's dialectal.

> Note: Why "shiran" means "don't know"
> You already know:
> - 知る (shiru) = to know
> - 知らない (shiranai) = don't know
>
> 知らん (shiran) is simply a casual contraction of 知らない.
> Think of it as:
> 知らない → しらん (shiran)
> A shortened, rougher, more colloquial version.

3) In feminine speech, you sometimes see: よ + わ → よわ. Example:

Sō yo wa.
そうよわ。
"That's right, you know."
This is old-fashioned and mostly literary or character-based now.

Just to be crystal clear, わ is not the same as は.
- は (wa) = topic marker (written は, pronounced わ)
- わ = sentence-ending particle

They are unrelated in function.

Yo ne よね:

It is not a separate particle. It is two particles used together: よ + ね → よね. They combine into a single unit of meaning, but grammatically they remain two particles stacked. It blends the functions of both particles:

- よ = assertion, giving information
- ね = seeking agreement, checking shared understanding

Together: よね = "I'm telling you this, and you agree… right?" It's assertive and cooperative at the same time.

1) Confirming something you believe is true.
Kore wa **oishii** yo ne.
これは**おいしい**よね。
This is **good**, right?

Nuance: You're asserting your opinion (よ) but also inviting agreement (ね).

2) Shared realization.
Are, kyō tte **yasumidatta** yo ne.
あれ、今日って**休みだった**よね。
Wait, today **was a holiday**, right?

Nuance: You think you're correct and want the listener to confirm.

3) Softening a strong opinion.
Ano **eiga**, sugoku yokatta yo ne.
あの**映画**、すごくよかったよね。
That **movie** was really good, wasn't it?

Nuance: You're stating your view but making space for the listener to join in.

よね is softer than よ but more assertive than ね.

PART III: QUESTIONS & UNCERTAINTY

Key stems and nuances in this section:

- ittai いったい → Intensifier in questions ("What on earth…?")
- ka か, noka のか → Direct questions, rhetorical reflection, feminine wondering

Vocabulary to review:

akeru	開ける	to open (door, window), to unwrap, to make something available
imi	意味	meaning, sense, significance
kamoshirenai	かもしれない	might / may / possibly
kimeru	決める	to decide / to choose / to determine / establish (a rule, plan, schedule, etc
kippu	切符	ticket
maniau	間に合う	to be in time / to be sufficient
oboeru	覚える	to remember, to memorize, to feel (sensation or emotion)
ryokō	旅行	trip
shikashi	しかし	however
shiraberu	調べる	to check, investigate, look up, examine or research
tashikameru	確かめる	to check, to confirm
tokoro ga	ところが	however, unexpectedly, contrary to what was expected
tsukeru	つける	to turn on (power), to apply, to soak, to add (flavor, label)
tsukuru	作る	to make, create, produce, prepare (food)
yaru	やる	to do
yoyaku	予約	to book (hotel/flight etc), to reserve

Diving further into the stems and nuances

Ittai (一体):

An adverb that adds emotional force to a question. It is purely an intensifier. Such as:

- What on earth…?

- Why in the world…?
- Who the heck…?
- How in the world…?

It expresses surprise, confusion, frustration, concern, or disbelief. It does not mean "but." Any sense of contrast comes from the context, not the word itself.

Why it might feel like "but" sometimes: いったい often appears in sentences where the speaker is emotionally pushing back against something unexpected or confusing. For example:

Ittai dō iu koto?
いったいどういうこと？
What on earth is going on?

The emotional pushback can feel like:

- "But… what is this?"
- "But… how did this happen?"

But that "but" feeling comes from the situation, not from the word いったい. It's the tone, not the meaning.

Compare with actual "but" words. Japanese has several true contrast markers:

- demo でも = but
- shikashi しかし = however
- kedo/ keredo けど / けれど = but / though
- noni のに = even though
- tokoro ga ところが = however (unexpected turn)

いったい is not in this family at all. It is almost always paired with a question word such as nani 何, dare 誰, dōshite どうして, dōiu どういう, doko どこ, or dō yatte どうやって.

Meaning of dōiu どういう:

At its core, どういう means:

- what kind of…
- what sort of…
- in what sense…
- what do you mean by…

It asks for clarification of meaning, not method (that's dō yatte どうやって) and not reason (that's dōshite どうして).
Think of it as the Japanese way of saying:
"What exactly do you mean?"

Examples to make it click:
1. Asking for clarification
Dō iu **imi** desu ka.
どういう**意味**ですか。
→ "What do you **mean**?"
→ "What kind of **meaning** is that?"

2. Asking about the nature of something
Dō iu **hito** ga suki desu ka.
どういう**人**が好きですか。
→ "What kind of **person** do you like?"

3. Expressing confusion
Dō iu koto?
どういうこと？
→ "What do you mean?"
→ "What's going on?"
→ "How does that make sense?"
This one is extremely common in conversation.

Meaning of dō yatte どうやって:
- How (in what way)…?
- By what method…?
- How exactly did you do that…?

It asks about the method, the procedure, or the means by which something is done.
It is not the same as doshite どうして ("why").
It is not the same as dō どう ("how" in a general sense).
It specifically targets the method.

Examples of ittai (一体) as an intensifier:

1. Confusion / "What on earth…?"
Ittai nani ga **okitan** desu ka.
いったい何が**起きたん**ですか。
What on earth **happened**?
This is the classic use: confusion + urgency.

2. Frustration / "Why in the world…?"
Ittai dōshite sonna koto o **iu** no.
いったいどうしてそんなことを**言う**の。
Why in the world would you **say** that?

Here, いったい adds emotional pressure.

3. Suspicion / "Who the heck…?"
Ittai **dare** ga konna koto o shitan da.
いったい**誰**がこんなことをしたんだ。
Who the heck did this?
This one carries a sharper, almost confrontational tone.

Ka - か:

A particle that marks questions, uncertainty, or alternatives. While beginners first learn か as a simple question marker, its deeper value lies in how it marks embedded questions, "whether" clauses, and rhetorical questions. These functions make it an essential part of the Japanese uncertainty system.

Side-note: The basic question marker. か marks a formal or neutral question:

Ikimasu ka.
行きますか。
Are you going?

In casual speech, か is often replaced by rising intonation or by の (no).

- か = formal, neutral, distant
- の = casual, softer, often used by women or in friendly speech

行くの？
Are you going? (casual)
行きますか。
Are you going? (polite)

Beyond simple questions, it signals unknown information inside a sentence and appears in rhetorical or emotional expressions.

1) Embedded questions (content questions inside a larger sentence). Here, か does not make the whole sentence a question. It marks the unknown information being talked about.

Nani o itta ka **oboete** inai.
何を言ったか**覚え**ていない。
I don't **remember** what he said.
Nuance: か marks the content of the question ("what he said").

2) "Whether / if" (かどうか). Used when the speaker is unsure between alternatives.

Iku ka dōka **kimete** inai.
行くかどうか**決めて**いない。
I haven't **decided** whether I'll go.

Nuance: か marks the uncertainty; どうか completes the "whether or not" structure.

3) Rhetorical or emotional questions. Often used in writing or strong speech where the speaker does not expect an answer.

Dare ga **shinjiru** mono ka.
誰が**信じる**ものか。
Who would **believe** that?

Dōshite **wakaru** mono ka.
どうして**分かる**ものか。
How could I possibly **know**?

Nuance: rejecting, emphatic, emotional.

Note: ものか / もんか (mono ka) is the key to the sentence's tone.

- mono here is the explanatory もの, but in this construction it becomes emphatic and emotional
- ka turns it into a rhetorical question
- Together, mono ka expresses:
- As if I would know!
- No way I'd know!
- How could I possibly know?

It's strong, dismissive, and often conveys irritation, disbelief, or rejection. This is not the same as the gentle explanatory んですか. This is the speaker pushing back.

4) Uncertainty in set expressions. か appears in several common uncertainty patterns:

- 〜かもしれない (〜kamoshirenai) — "might / maybe"

Ame ga furu kamoshirenai.
雨が降るかもしれない。
It might **rain**.

Kare wa mō **kaetta** kamoshirenai.
彼はもう**帰った**かもしれない。
He might have already **gone home**.

Maniawanai kamoshirenai.
間に合わないかもしれない。
I might **not make it in time**.

Note: かもしれない is built from three components, and none of them function as a "base verb" the way asobu 遊ぶ or taberu 食べる do. かもしれない comes from か (uncertainty) + も (even) + 知れない (cannot know), but in modern Japanese it functions as a single expression meaning "might / maybe." Moreover, 知れない (shirenai) "cannot know" comes from the negative potential of 知る (shiru), which is "to know."

- ～かな (～kana) — "I wonder…" (casual)

Examples:
Ashita, **hareru** kana.
明日、**晴れる**かな。
I wonder if **it'll be sunny** tomorrow.

Kare, kuru kana…
彼、来るかな...
I wonder if he'll come…

Kore de ii no kana.
これでいいのかな。
I wonder if this is okay.

- ～かどうか (～ka dō ka) — "whether or not"

Iku ka dōka mada **kimete** inai.
行くかどうかまだ**決めて**いない。
I haven't **decided** whether I'll go.

Kare ga **kuru** ka dōka wakaranai.
彼が**来る**かどうか分からない。
I don't know whether he's **coming**.

Hontō ka dōka **tashikamete** kudasai.
本当かどうか**確かめて**ください。
Please **check** whether it's true.

These show how か participates in expressing doubt or possibility.

No ka のか:

A sentence-ending construction (の + か). Adds a tone of uncertainty, wondering, or emotional questioning. Softer and more reflective than simply ending with か. Think of のか as: "Is it that…?" "I wonder if…?" "Why is it that…?" It's not a neutral question — it carries feeling.

1) Genuine uncertainty / wondering

Dōshite konna koto ni natta no ka.
どうしてこんなことになったのか。
I wonder how things ended up like this.
This is not a direct question to someone — it's internal, reflective.

2) Seeking an explanation ("Why is it that…?")

Naze kare wa **konai** no ka.
なぜ彼は**来ない**のか。
Why is it that he **isn't coming**?
This is stronger than a simple "Why isn't he coming?" It implies frustration or confusion.

> Why do we have both なぜ and のか in the same sentence? Because なぜ asks what the question is about, and のか **expresses** the emotional tone of the question. They do different jobs, so they can appear together without repeating meaning.
>
> なぜ = "why" (the question word)
> It tells you what information the speaker wants.
> ✓ のか = "Is it that…?" / "Why is it that…?"
> It adds tone:
> - wondering
> - confusion
> - frustration
> - emotional questioning
> - seeking explanation

It does not replace the question word.
It shapes the feeling of the question.

3) Emotional questioning (surprise, disbelief, frustration)

Nande watashi ga **yaru** no ka.
なんで私が**やる**のか。
Why is it that I have **to do** it?

The のか adds emotional weight — annoyance, disbelief, or protest.

Why does yaru (やる = to do) appear in this sentence? This is one of those sentences where the literal grammar and the natural English meaning don't line up neatly. Once you see the structure, the nuance becomes obvious. Let's break it down and see why the natural translation becomes "Why me, of all people?"

Breakdown of なんで私がやるのか

a) なんで (nande)
Here it means "why" (the reason why) or "for what reason."
Not "how," not "with what" — this is the "why" usage.

b) 私が (watashi ga)
This is the key to the nuance.

- 私 (watashi) = I / me
- が (ga) = subject marker, but here it adds contrast or focus

In emotional questioning, X が often means: "Why me?" "Why do I have to do it?" This is where the "of all people" nuance comes from.

c) やる (yaru)
"To do (it)."
A plain, direct, casual verb: "to be the one who does it."

d) のか (no ka)
Adds emotional questioning: frustration, disbelief, protest, "Why is it that…?", "How come…?"
It's not a neutral question — it carries feeling.

Literal reading:
"Why is it that I am the one who has to do it?"

Natural English:
"Why me, of all people?"

Why does English add "of all people"? Because English needs extra words to express the contrastive focus that Japanese expresses with 私が.

4) Soft rhetorical question

Hontō ni kore de ii no ka.
本当にこれでいいのか。
Is this **really** okay?

This is not a literal question — it's self-checking or doubting.

のか (no ka) is two separate concepts, not a single word. のか = の + か (two concepts working together)

- の → explanatory / emotional / "the reason that…"
- か → question marker

When combined, they create a questioning or wondering tone, but they never fuse into a single lexical item.

Note: In romaji, のか should be written as two separate words: no ka.
Why?
Because:

- の and か are two separate grammatical units
- They never fuse into a single particle
- They each keep their own function (explanatory の + question か)

So even though they feel like one unit when spoken, they are not one word in Japanese grammar.

✓ Correct romaji

- no ka

✗ Incorrect romaji

- noka (don't write it this way)

Part IV: EXPLANATORY & CAUSAL

Key stems and nuances in this section:

- ～te-oku ～ておく → functions as a helper verb when attached to the て-form.
- datte だって, kara から, kedo けど, koto こと, mono もの, no の, node ので, noni のに, shi し, wake わけ, → Reasons, justifications, explanatory tone
- ga が, kedo けど, keredo けれど(も) → Contrastive connectors
- ki 気 → feelings, mood, intention, energy, atmosphere, the "air" of a situation
- kuse ni くせに → "Even though…" with critical nuance
- nan なん, ndesu んです, no desu のです → explanation, background, softening, inviting understanding
- shi し → Listing reasons
- shite して → Conjunctive form, linking clauses

Vocabulary to review:

abiru	浴びる	to bathe in, to pour over oneself, to be exposed to (light, water, attention, etc.)
ageru	あげる	to give (to someone else)
ame	雨	rain
anshin	安心	peace of mind
atsui	暑い	hot
chigau	ちがう	to differ / to be different
chikai	近い	near, close by
chizu	地図	map
daremo	だれも	nobody, no one / everyone, anybody (depending on polarity)
dasu	出す	movement outward / literal (take out), abstract (submit), or emotional (burst out laughing)
dekakeru	出かける	to go out, to leave home
dekiru	できる	can, able to do
denki	電気	electricity
eki	駅	train station
erasō (comes from erai)	えらそう	acting important or superior, full of oneself, pretentious
hajimaru	始まる	to start, it begins

hareru	晴れる	to clear up (as in weather improves) / paired with "ki" 気 = emotional relief
hataraku (verb)	働く	to perform work, to labor, to be employed
hayaku	早く	quickly, fast, early
hiku	引く	to pull / to subside
hikkosu	引っ越す	to move (from one dwelling to another)
hima	暇	free (time), not busy
itadaku	いただく	to receive, to accept, to be able to receive
iwareru	言われる	to be told
jijō	事情	circumstances, situation, reasons, or conditions
jōzu	上手	skillful, good at, proficient
jinsei	人生	life
kangaekata	考え方	way of thinking
kansha	感謝	gratitude, thanks
kantan	簡単	easy
kawaru	変わる	to change, to shift, to become different, to switch (roles, states, conditions)
kieru	消える	disappeared
kikoeru	聞こえる	to be audible (sound naturally reaches you)
kimi	君	you (casual)
kimochi	気持ち	feeling
kirai	嫌い	dislike
kiri	霧	fog
kiru	着る	to wear (clothes)
kodomo	子ども	child
kokoro	心	heart
kowai	怖い（こわい）	scary, afraid
kuchi	口	mouth
machigaeru	間違える	to make a mistake, get it wrong, to misidentify
majime	真面目	serious
mama	まま	as is / maintaining a state
mazu	まず	first (of all), before anything else, anyway / at any rate

mechakucha	めちゃくちゃ	extremely, ridiculously, absurdly, chaotic/messed up, out of control
minna	みんな	everyone
monku	文句	complaint
mōshiwake	申し訳	excuse, explanation, justification, reason offered to account for something
muri	無理	impossible, can't do it, too much
muzukashii	難しい	difficult
naoru	治る	it will heal
neru	寝る	to go to bed, to sleep
ninki	人気	popular, popularity
okiru	起きる	to wake up, to get up
omoshiroi	面白い	interesting
ōi	多い	many
oshieru	教える	to teach, to tell, to inform, to show (how to do something)
owaru	終わる	to end, to finish, to come to an end
raigetsu	来月	next month
renshū	練習	practice
saikin	最近	lately, recently
saikō	最高	the best
saki	先	the point that lies "ahead" of something; in time, space, order, or position
setsumei (noun)	説明	explanation, justification, a description, or instructions
shashin	写真	photograph
shigoto (noun)	仕事	work, job, occupation, task, the thing you do as work
shiru	知る	to know, to find out
sorotta	揃った	all present
sumu	住む	to live, reside
takai	高い	tall, expensive
tanoshii	楽しい	fun
ten	点	points, score, grade, mark
tetsudau	手伝う	to help / to assist
totemo	とても	very
tsukareru	疲れる	to get tired, exhausted

tsukau	使う	to use / to spend (money)
umai	うまい	good
undou	運動	exercise
urusai	うるさい	noisy / bothersome / annoying / shut up! / overly particular
yaseru	痩せる	lose weight
yoroshii	よろしい	good, acceptable, permissible, that will do / very well (formal acceptance)
yuki	雪	snow
yurusu	許す	to permit, allow, forgive
zenbu	全部	all

Diving further into the stems and nuances

～te-oku (～ておく):

This construction comes from the verb 置く (oku) meaning "to place / to put," but in this grammar pattern it has become a grammaticalized auxiliary. It no longer means "to place something physically." Instead, it expresses doing something in advance, preparing, or leaving something as is. Linguistically, this is often described as a "preparatory aspect" because it marks an action performed now for future benefit. It expresses foresight, convenience, or intentional maintenance of a state. In casual speech, it often contracts to ～とく (～ toku) / ～どく (～ doku).

1) Doing something in advance (preparation) is the primary meaning. You perform an action now so that things will be easier or smoother later.

Kippu o katte oku.
切符を買っておく。
I'll buy the **ticket** ahead of time.

Bangohan o **tsukutte** oita.
晩ごはんを**作って**おいた。
I **made** dinner in advance.

Ryokō no mae ni hoteru o yoyaku shite okimasu.
旅行の前にホテルを予約しておきます。
I'll book the hotel before the **trip**.

Nuance: preparation, foresight, planning.

2) Leaving something as it is / maintaining a state. You intentionally don't change something. You leave it in its current condition for a reason.

Doa wa **akete** oite.
ドアは**開けて**おいて。
Leave the door **open**.

Sono mama ni shite oite kudasai.
そのままにしておいてください。
Please leave it as it is.

Note: "Sono mama" means "in that state."

Denki wa tsukete oite ii yo.
電気はつけておいていいよ。
You can leave the **light** on.
Nuance: purposeful non-interference.

3) Doing something for later benefit (self or others). This overlaps with "in advance," but the nuance is more about future convenience than preparation.

Memo shite oku ne.
メモしておくね。
I'll jot it down (so I don't forget later).

Basho o shirabete oita yo.
場所を調べておいたよ。
I looked up the **place** for you (so you'll be ready).

Nuance: helpfulness, foresight, convenience.

A note on casual contractions

In speech, ～ておく often contracts:
- ～とく (from ～ておく)
- ～どく (from ～でおく)

Examples:
Nomu + de oku → nondo ku
飲んどく？
Should I drink it now to get it out of the way?

Yondoku yo.
読んどくよ。
I'll read it ahead of time.

These are extremely common in casual conversation.

Datte (だって):

A word used to give reasons, justifications, explanations, or emotional reactions. It can function like "because," "but," "even," or "after all," depending on context. It often appears at the start of a sentence to introduce an excuse, a reason, or a protest. It does not behave like a normal particle; rather, it's closer to an explanatory connector or emotional preface.

1) Giving a reason / excuse ("because…"). This is the most common use in conversation. だって introduces the speaker's justification, often with a slightly defensive or emotional tone.

<u>Datte</u> **samui** n da mon.
<u>だって</u>**寒い**んだもん。
"<u>Because</u> it's **cold**." / "But it's **cold**!"

> Note: Mon (もん) is a sentence-ending explanatory/emotional particle. It adds: justification, personal reasoning, emotional tone, a slightly childlike or defensive flavor. It's closely related to もの (mono), but もん is the softer, more casual, more emotional version. もの is discussed in detail later in this section. Here is a brief summary:

Form	Tone	Usage
もの	more formal, neutral	written, adult speech
もん	softer, emotional, childlike	casual, spoken

> So in 寒いんだもん (samui n da mon), the speaker isn't just saying: "It's cold." They're saying: "It's cold, that's why!" "But it's cold!" "It's because it's cold!"

> Important note: もん ≠ an exclamation mark. An exclamation mark shows volume or force in English. But もん shows emotional justification, a reason with feelings attached. It's not about shouting. It's about defending, explaining, or protesting.

Datte **shiranakatta** n da yo.
だって**知らなかった**んだよ。
"I mean, I **didn't know**."

Ikenai yo. Datte **shigoto** ga arun da.
行けないよ。だって**仕事**があるんだ。
"I can't go. Because I have **work**."

Nuance: soft, emotional, often used when explaining oneself.

2) "Even…" (emphatic highlighting). だって can mean "even" when placed before a noun or phrase. This usage emphasizes something surprising or extreme.

Datte kodomo da yo.
だって子どもだよ。
"He's just a kid, you know."

Watashi datte dekiru yo.
私だってできるよ。
"Even I can do it!"

Kare datte wakatteru yo.
彼だって分かってるよ。
"Even he understands."

Nuance: emphasis, highlighting, "even X…"

3) Softening or prefacing an explanation ("well… / you see…"). だって can act like a gentle lead-in before giving background or context.

Datte ne, kinō **attan** da yo.
だってね、昨日**会ったん**だよ。
"Well, you see, I **met** him yesterday."

Datte sa, **kyū** ni iwaretan da mon. (See explanation for "mon" in previous page.)
だってさ、**急に**言われたんだもん。
"Well, you know, they told me **suddenly**."
Nuance: conversational softener, often paired with ね or さ.

4) Quoting or reporting ("they say… / I heard…"). In casual speech, だって can introduce reported information, similar to ～って.

Ashita, ame datte.
明日、雨だって。
"They say it'll rain tomorrow."

Kare, **konai** n datte.
彼、**来ない**んだって。
"I heard he's **not coming**."
Nuance: hearsay, casual reporting.

5) Childlike or emotional protest ("But…!"). Very common in children's speech or playful adult speech.

Datte iya nan da mon!
だってイヤなんだもん！
"But I don't wanna!"

> Note: もん (mon) is the emotional もの, used especially by: children, young women, or anyone speaking in a cute, pouty, or defensive tone. It adds:
> - insistence
> - emotional justification
> - "That's why!" / "Because that's how it is!"
>
> So "nan da mon" = It's because I don't like it, okay?!"

Datte **kowai** n da yo!
だって**怖い**んだよ！
"But it's **scary**!"

Nuance: emotional, whiny, cute, playful or dramatic.

Ga (が):

The explanatory & contrastive connector. The core ideas are "but / although / however," a soft, polite connector that introduces contrast, background, or an explanation. Unlike けど or けれど, が is more formal and more neutral. It appears in: polite conversation, written Japanese, softening statements, introducing background before the main point.

1) Simple contrast ("but"). This is the most common meaning.

Ame ga futte iru ga, **dekakenakya ikenai**.
雨が降っているが、**出かけなきゃいけない**。
It's raining, but **I have (must) to go out**.

Note: Nakya なきゃ does not mean "must." It only means "if (I) don't…" The "must" meaning only appears when なきゃ is followed by ikenai いけない / naranai ならない / dame だめ. So:

- dekakenakya 出かけなきゃ
  = if I don't go out… (incomplete)
- dekakenakya ikenai 出かけなきゃいけない
  = I must go out
  (literally: if I don't go out, it won't do)

Kono hon wa **takai** ga, totemo omoshiroi.
この本は**高い**が、とても面白い。
This book is **expensive**, but very interesting.

Nuance: Neutral, factual contrast. Softer and more formal than けど.

2) Softening / polite preface ("…but…"). が is often used to soften a request, question, or refusal. In English, this "but" often disappears.

Sumimasen ga, chotto **tetsudatte** itadakemasu ka.
すみませんが、ちょっと**手伝って**いただけますか。
Excuse me, could you **help me**?

Side-note: Why itadakemasu (いただけます) doesn't translate directly to English? いただけます is the polite potential form of いただく, a humble verb meaning "to receive." But in the pattern ～ていただけますか, it **does not** mean "receive" in the English sense. Instead, it adds a humble, polite nuance to the action before it.

How it works:

- tetsudatte 手伝って = "help (me)"
- itadakemasu ka いただけますか = "is it possible for me to receive (your action)?"

Put together:
手伝っていただけますか
= "Could I receive your helping?"
→ natural English: "Could you help me?"

The English translation drops the "receive" idea entirely, but the Japanese politeness comes from it.

Why this matters…
The speaker is not just asking for help —
they are humbly receiving the other person's effort.

Mōshiwake arimasen ga, kyō wa ikemasen.
申し訳ありませんが、今日は行けません。
I'm sorry (there is no excuse), but I can't go today.

Nuance: が here doesn't express strong contrast. It's a politeness buffer.

Note: Mōshiwake arimasen (申し訳ありません) is NOT the negative of "I'm sorry." It is a set humble expression meaning:

- "I'm terribly sorry."
- "I sincerely apologize."
- "I have no excuse."

The ありません here does not negate the apology. It negates the excuse.
Literally:

- mōshiwake 申し訳 = excuse / justification
- arimasen ありません = there is none

So the literal meaning is:
"There is no excuse."
And culturally, that equals:
"I am deeply sorry."
This is why the negative form is required. It's part of the fixed humble apology.

3) Background → main point ("although…"). が can introduce background information before the real message.

Kinō wa isogashikatta ga, kyō wa **jikan** ga aru.
昨日は忙しかったが、今日は**時間**がある。
I was busy yesterday, but today I have **time**.

Setsumei shitai koto ga aru ga, mazu kore o mite kudasai.
説明したいことがあるが、まずこれを見てください。
There's something I want to **explain**, but first please look at this.

Nuance: Sets up context before the main clause.

Note: Setsumei 説明 means more than just "explanation." Depending on context, it can also mean a justification, a description, or instructions. Anything that involves making something clear.

Note: Even though ～tai (～たい) is technically an adjective form, the entire phrase setsumei shitai (説明したい) still functions as a relative clause modifying the noun koto (こと). Because a verb/adjective clause cannot attach directly to the existence marker が ある, it must modify a noun like koto (thing/matter).

This is why Japanese says "Setsumei shitai koto ga aru" (説明したいことがある), not "Setsumei shitai ga aru" (説明したいがある.)

4) が at the end of a sentence (soft trailing "but…"). In conversation, が can appear at the end of a sentence, leaving the rest implied. This is extremely common in polite speech.

Chotto **onegai** ga arun desu ga…
ちょっと**お願い**があるんですが...
I have a small **favor** to ask, but…

Side-note: This sentence contains two completely different が's, each with its own function:
1) が as the subject marker
お願いがある
= "There is a request (I have a favor)."
Here, が marks お願い as the subject of ある. This is the standard grammatical が.

2) が as a soft, trailing connector ("but…")
…んですが
= "but…" / "however…" (softening the transition)
This が is not a subject marker. It's the conjunctive が, used to gently lead into the main point or request. It softens the tone, making the sentence polite and indirect.

Oisogashii tokoro **kyōshuku** desu ga, ima yoroshii deshō ka.
お忙しいところ**恐縮**ですが、今よろしいでしょうか。
I'm sorry to bother you when you're busy, but is now a good time?

Nuance: Soft, indirect, polite. The listener understands the unspoken continuation.

5) が vs. けど (kedo) / けれど (keredo).
All of these can mean "but," but their tone differs:

- が — formal, neutral, often used in polite speech and writing. Softens statements.
- けど — casual, conversational, can carry emotion or personal feeling.
- けれど / けれども — more formal than けど, softer than が, common in polite conversation.

Key idea:
が is the most neutral and polite.
けど is casual and emotional.
けれど sits in the middle.

Kara (から):

A particle with several core meanings. Its two most common functions are:

- marking a **starting point** (time, place, range)
- expressing a **reason or cause** ("because…")

It also appears in a few structural and idiomatic patterns.

1) Starting point (time or place). Marks where something begins; a time, a location. It also sets a range (kara / made). から marks the starting point; まで marks the ending point.

Examples Using Time:
San-ji kara **hajimaru**.
３時から始まる。
It **starts** from three o'clock.

Ashita kara **shigoto** da.
明日から仕事だ。
I start **work** from tomorrow.

> Side-note:
> shigoto 仕事 = the work itself (job, duties, tasks).
> Hataraku 働く = the act of working.
> Neither means "workplace," that's shokuba 職場 or kaisha 会社.

Example Using Location:
Eki kara aruita.
駅から歩いた。
I walked from the **station**.

Examples Using Range (kara / made):

Eki kara ie made aruita.
駅から家まで歩いた。
I walked from the **station** to the house. (Location)

Ku-ji kara go-ji made **hataraku**.
９時から５時まで**働く**。
I **work** from 9 to 5. (Time)

Koko kara soko made ga watashi no **hatake** desu.
ここからそこまでが私の**畑**です。
From here to there is my **field**. (Range)

Nuance: neutral, factual, extremely common.

2) Reason / cause ("because…"). から attaches to the end of a clause to explain why something happened or why the speaker feels a certain way.

Plain form + から
Samui kara, kōto o **kita**.
寒いから、コートを**着た**。
Because it's cold, I **wore** a coat.

> Side-note: Although spelled the same way in romaji (kita), this past-tense form can mean either "came" or "wore" depending on the kanji.
> - 来た comes from 来る (kuru) — "to come."
> - 着た comes from 着る (kiru) — "to wear (clothes)."

Isogashii kara ikenai.
忙しいから行けない。
I can't go because I'm **busy**.

Polite form + から
Jikan ga nai desu kara, **saki** ni ikimasu.
時間がないですから、**先**に行きます。
Because I don't have time, I'll go **ahead**.

Nuance: straightforward reason; slightly more direct than ので; common for personal explanations.

3) ～te kara (～てから) = "after doing…" Indicates a sequence: Action A → then Action B). Focuses on **order**, not the time gap.

Gohan o tabete kara benkyō suru.
ご飯を食べてから勉強する。
I'll study after eating.

> Side-note: Beginners may already know the phrase "ato de" (あとで), which means later, and may question why あとで is not used in the example above. あとで = sometime later, often with a looser sense of time (not necessarily immediately). It doesn't imply a tight sequence. This can mean:
>
> - right after eating
> - or an hour later
> - or sometime later in the day
>
> ～てから implies Action A must finish before Action B can happen. あとで simply means Action B happens at a later point in time.

Ie ni kaette kara shawā o **abita**.
家に帰ってからシャワーを**浴びた**。
After getting home, I **took a shower**.

Nuance: clear sequence; no emotional tone.

4) "Since…" (starting point in time → continuing effect). Similar to English "ever since."

Nihon ni kite kara, Nihongo ga **jōzu** ni natta.
日本に来てから、日本語が**上手**になった。
Since coming to Japan, my Japanese has **improved**.

Kare to atte kara, kangaekata ga **kawatta**.
彼と会ってから、考え方が**変わった**。
Since meeting him, my way of thinking **changed**.

Nuance: starting point → ongoing effect.

> Side-note: Why 考え方 (kangaekata) means "way of thinking." The noun 考え (kangae) means: a thought, an idea, thinking (as a concept). The suffix ～方 (kata) means: the way of doing something, the method / manner / style. It attaches to the stem of a verb to create a noun meaning "how to ___."
> So:

- 考える (kangaeru) = to think
- 考え = thought / thinking
- 考え方 = the way of thinking. (Literally: "thinking-method")

This is the same pattern as:

- 読み方 (yomikata) = way of reading
- 使い方 (tsukaikata) = way of using
- 書き方 (kakikata) = way of writing
- 言い方 (iikata) = way of saying

5) Perspective / basis ("from the standpoint of…")

A) ～kara miru to (～から見ると). Objective / observational viewpoint. (When seen from X's point of view.)

Sensei kara miru to, kare wa **majime** da.
先生から見ると、彼は**真面目**だ。
From the teacher's point of view, he's **serious**.

Side-note: Where "point of view" comes from. Japanese expresses point of view by combining miru (見る) with a source marker like kara (から):
～から見ると
"from the point of view of…"
"when seen from…"

見ると without から. When used alone, 見ると means:

- "when you look at it…"
- "if you look…"
- "upon seeing…"

For example:
Chizu o miru to, koko wa chikai.
地図を見ると、ここは近い。
Looking at the **map**, this place is nearby.

B) ～kara shitara (～からしたら). Subjective / empathetic viewpoint. Imagining how X feels or experiences something.

Kodomo kara shitara, kore wa **muzukashii** yo.
子どもからしたら、これは**難しい**よ。
From a child's perspective, this is **hard**.

Nuance: imagining X's feelings or standpoint.

C) ～kara suru to (～からすると). Analytical / inferential viewpoint. Used when drawing a conclusion from evidence or clues.

Kare no **taido** kara suru to, okotte iru to omou.
彼の**態度**からすると、怒っていると思う。
Judging from his **attitude**, I think he's angry.
Nuance: slightly more formal or analytical.

Compact summary between the three viewpoints:

Pattern	Viewpoint Type	Core Meaning
～kara miru to ～から見ると	objective, observational (based on looking)	"when seen from…"
～kara shitara ～からしたら	subjective, empathetic (based on feeling)	"from X's standpoint…"
～kara suru to ～からすると	analytical, inferential (based on evidence)	"judging from…"

Kedo (けど) / Keredo (けれど) / Keredomo (けれども):

These three forms all mean "but / although / however." The difference is not strict politeness — it's tone, softness, and formality. Think of them as the same meaning expressed with different levels of length and smoothness.

1) Kedo けど is the most casual, conversational. Short, light, and extremely common in everyday speech. Often softens statements or trails off politely.

Ikitai kedo, **okane** ga nai.
行きたいけど、**お金**がない。
I want to go, but I don't have **money**.

> Side-note: 金 (kane) already means "money." お is an honorific prefix that makes it polite and natural. In conversation, people almost always say お金.

2) Keredo けれど is semi-formal, neutral-polite. Slightly more formal than けど, but not stiff. Common in polite conversation, writing, and narration.

Ikitai keredo, kyō wa **isogashii** desu.
行きたいけれど、今日は**忙しい**です。
I want to go, but I'm **busy** today.

3) Keredomo けれども is the most formal and emphatic, longest and softest. Used in formal writing, speeches, or when adding weight or care to the contrast. The も adds a gentle emphasis.

Ikitai keredomo, **jijō** ga yurushimasen.
行きたいけれども、**事情**が許しません。
I want to go; however, **circumstances** do not permit it.

Compact summary:

Form	Tone	Usage
kedo けど	casual, light	everyday speech
keredo けれど	neutral, polite	polite conversation, writing
keredemo けれども	formal, gentle, emphatic	speeches, careful writing

---

Ki 気:

In Japanese, 気 (ki) is one of the most important and wide-reaching concepts in the language. At its core, 気 refers to the invisible inner world — feelings, mood, intention, energy, atmosphere, awareness, and even the "air" of a situation. It's the part of human experience that can't be touched but can always be felt. Because of this, 気 appears in hundreds of expressions, each capturing a different shade of human emotion or mental state:

- genki 元気 — vitality, health, spirit
- ki ga au – 気が合う — to get along
- ki ga hareru – 気が晴れる — to feel emotionally cleared
- ki ga omoi – 気が重い — to feel weighed down
- ki ga suru – 気がする — to have a feeling that…
- ki ga tsuku – 気がつく — to notice
- ki ni naru – 気になる — something occupies your mind
- ki ni iru – 気に入る — to like something
- ki wo tsukeru – 気をつける — to be mindful / careful
- kibun 気分 — mood
- kimochi 気持ち — feeling

In all of these, 気 acts like a container for the mind, heart, and atmosphere — the "weather" inside a person. And just like real weather, that inner atmosphere can be bright, cloudy, heavy, scattered, calm, or stormy.

Japanese uses 気 the way English uses "mind," "spirit," "mood," "energy," and "intuition," but it's broader than any one of those words. It's a cultural lens: a way of describing the subtle emotional currents that shape human behavior.

A Note on the Kanji: 気 vs. 木

Although 気 (ki) means "energy," "spirit," or "feeling," there is another word pronounced ki that means "tree" — written with a completely different kanji:

- 木 (ki) — tree, wood

These two words sound identical but have no connection in meaning. This is a common feature of Japanese: same pronunciation, different kanji, different meaning. So:

- 気 = spirit, energy, mood
- 木 = tree, wood

Learners often confuse them at first, but the kanji make the meaning clear.

Koto こと:

A noun that turns actions, events, and experiences into "things." It has two major grammatical functions:

A. Nominalizer: turns a verb phrase or clause into a noun-like unit ("the act of…," "the fact that…").

B. Abstract "thing": refers to intangible things such as experiences, rules, general matters, or facts.

Beginners often learn "koto = thing," but in practice it means an abstract, non-physical thing, unlike もの, which refers to concrete or conceptualized things.

1) Nominalizer (turning actions into nouns). Used mid-sentence to treat an action or state as a "thing." Examples:

Nihongo o benkyō suru koto wa **tanoshii.**
日本語を勉強することは**楽しい**。
Studying Japanese is fun.
(literally: "The thing of studying Japanese is **fun**.")

Sidebar: Why Japanese treats actions as "things."

Japanese grammar often requires a noun-like unit in positions where English allows a full clause. For example, the particle は (a topic marker) **can only attach to nouns or nominalized phrases, <u>not to raw verbs</u>.**

So if you want to say: "Studying Japanese is fun" **you need the subject to be a noun.** English allows "Studying" (a gerund). Japanese **does not allow** "benkyō suru" 勉強

する to function as a noun by itself. That's why Japanese uses: benkyō suru koto 勉強すること "the act of studying." It turns the verb phrase into a thing, so it can function grammatically as the topic or subject.

Here's another way to look at this. Can't I simply say:
Nihongo o benkyou suru wa tanoshii.
日本語を勉強するは楽しい。

This is ungrammatical because:

- する is a verb
- **は cannot attach directly to a verb**
- Japanese needs a nominalizer to make the clause into a noun-like unit

So the correct form is:
Nihongo o benkyō suru koto wa **tanoshii**.
日本語を勉強することは**楽しい**。
Studying Japanese is **fun**.

End Sidebar

Asa hayaku **okiru** koto ga dekinai.
朝早く**起きる**ことができない。
I can't **wake up** early in the morning.
(literally: The act of waking up early in the morning is something I cannot do.")

Kare ga kuru koto o **shitte ita**.
彼が来ることを**知っていた**。
I **knew** that he would come.
(literally: "the fact that he will come")

Nuance: こと nominalizes actions, events, facts, and general truths — anything abstract.

2) Abstract "thing" (intangible matters, experiences, rules). Used as a standalone noun meaning "matter," "thing (non-physical)," "experience," or "fact."

Examples:
Ii koto o **oshiete ageru**.
いいことを**教えてあげる**。
I'll tell you something good.
("good information / good tip" — not a physical object)

Note: Ageru あげる means "to give," and when used after a te-form oshiete ageru (教えてあげる), it adds the nuance of doing the action for someone else's benefit.

Note: Oshiete 教えて is the te-form used as a request, so it already implies "tell me / teach me." In conversation, the "please" is implied. Without "ageru" the sentence becomes "tell me something good." So:

- oshiete 教えて = "tell me"
- oshiete ageru 教えてあげる = "I'll tell *you* (as a favor)"

They point in opposite directions.

Jinsei de <u>taisetsu</u> na koto wa nan desu ka.
人生で<u>大切</u>なことは何ですか。
What is <u>important</u> in **life**?
("important matters," not objects)

Shiranai koto ga <u>ōi</u>.
知らないことが<u>多い</u>。
There are <u>many</u> things I **don't know**.
("unknown facts")

3) ～ koto ga aru (～ことがある) / ～ koto ni suru (～ことにする) / ～ koto ni naru (～ことになる) (set expressions). These are extremely common patterns where こと forms part of a fixed grammatical structure.

A) ～ことがある — "there are times when…" / "have ever…"

Nihon de **yuki** o miru <u>koto ga aru</u>.
日本で**雪**を見る<u>ことがある</u>。
<u>Sometimes</u> I see **snow** in Japan.

Note: While some learners may know words that mean "sometimes" (tokidoki ときどき, tamani たまに, tokiniwa ときには, etc.), the ～ことがある structure itself expresses:

- "there are times when…"
- "sometimes…"
- "occasionally…"
- "have the experience of…"

It doesn't contain the word "sometimes," but the meaning is built into the grammar: the verb phrase becomes a "thing" (こと), and ある states that this "thing" happens at times.

Nihon ni itta koto ga aru.
日本に行ったことがある。
I have been to Japan before.

B) ～ことにする — "decide to…"

Mainichi **hashiru** koto ni shita.
毎日**走る**ことにした。
I decided to **run** every day.

C) ～ことになる — "it has been decided that…" / "it turns out that…"

Raigetsu hikkosu koto ni natta.
来月引っ越すことになった。
It's been decided that I'll move **next month**.

A quick comparison:
koto こと vs mono もの:

- こと = abstract "thing" (fact, idea, experience, rule, action)
- もの = concrete or conceptualized "thing" (object, event you can picture)

Kuse ni くせに:

A conjunctive phrase meaning: "even though… (and I'm annoyed about it)." Emotional tone: criticism, blame, irritation, calling out hypocrisy, or resentment. The word くせに connects two clauses where the second clause contradicts what you would normally expect from the first, and the speaker feels negatively about that contradiction. It is stronger and more judgmental than のに.

Note: Why the romaji is written separately ("kuse ni"). Romaji spacing follows morphology, not grammar function.

- kuse = a noun ("habit," "flaw," "tendency")
- ni = a particle

So in romaji, you naturally write: kuse ni. Just like you write: no ni, wake de, tame ni, wari ni. Even though each of these functions as a single grammatical connector, romaji still separates the pieces because they are originally separate words.

But in grammar, くせに is treated as ONE item. Even though it's written as two words in romaji, くせに is a fixed conjunctive phrase with a single meaning. Learners should memorize it as くせに, not as "kuse" by itself.
This is exactly like:

- のに
- わけで
- ために
- わりに

All of which are written as two romaji words but function as one grammar pattern.

1) Criticism / blame ("even though… you still…").

Kodomo no kuse ni, erisō na koto o **iu**.
子どものくせに、えらそうなことを**言う**。
Even though he's just a kid, he **talks** like he's so important.

Nani mo shiranai kuse ni, kuchi o dasu na.
何も知らないくせに、口を出すな。
Don't butt in when you don't know **anything**.
(Literally: Even though you don't know **anything**, don't put your mouth out.)
Nuance: calling out behavior, criticizing someone for acting above their status or ability.

Note: 何も (nanimo) literally means "anything," but when used with a negative verb (which is almost always), it means "nothing." Japanese expresses "nothing" as "anything + negative verb."

Note: 出す (dasu) means to take out, put out, send out, produce, or begin doing (when used as Verb-stem + 出す). The core idea is "movement outward," whether literal (take out), abstract (submit), or emotional (burst out laughing).
In 口を出す (kuchi o dasu), 出す keeps its literal "put out" meaning, but metaphorically extends to "stick your mouth in," which naturally becomes "interfere."

2) Hypocrisy / contradiction ("you act like… but actually…").

Benkyō shinai kuse ni, tesuto no ten ni **monku** o iu.
勉強しないくせに、テストの点に**文句**を言う。
He **complains** about his test score even though he doesn't study.

Kirei na kuse ni, **heya** wa mechakucha da.
きれいなくせに、**部屋**はめちゃくちゃだ。
She's beautiful, but her **room** is a total mess. (= "You'd expect better from her.")
Nuance: pointing out a mismatch between expectation and behavior.

3) Self-directed frustration ("even though I…").

Yaseru tte itta kuse ni, mata kēki tabeta.
痩せるって言ったくせに、またケーキ食べた。
Even though I said I'd **lose weight**, I ate cake again.

> Note: って (tte) is the casual form of the quoting particle と (to). In 痩せるって言ったくせに (Yaseru tte itta kuse ni), it quotes the phrase 痩せる / yaseru ("lose weight"). So the meaning is: Even though I said "I'd lose weight…" In other words, you are quoting your own (or someone else's) words.

Nuance: mild self-blame, regret, annoyance at oneself.

4) くせに with nouns and na-adjectives. Just like のに, くせに requires な before nouns and na-adjectives.

Gakusei na kuse ni, **okane** o tsukaisugi da.
学生なくせに、**お金**を使いすぎだ。
He's a student, yet he spends too much **money**.

> Note: 使いすぎ (tsukaisugi) means "overspending / using too much." It comes from 使う (tsukau) + すぎる (sugiru) = to overdo / to do too much. The form 使いすぎ is the noun / nominalized version of 使いすぎる, and in this sentence it functions as a predicate noun (〜だ).

Shizuka na kuse ni, hito no mae de wa urusai.
静かなくせに、人の前ではうるさい。
She's **quiet**, but she gets loud in front of people.

Mono もの:

A noun that serves two major grammatical functions:

1) As a nominalizer, it turns a clause into a "thing" (mid-sentence).

2) As an explanatory ending, it adds a personal, justifying, or reason-giving tone when used at the end of a sentence.

What is a "nominalizer"?
A nominalizer turns an action or clause into a noun-like idea so you can talk about it as a "thing." Think of it like this:

- run → an action
- the act of running → a noun-like thing
- eat → an action
- what you ate → a noun-like thing

Japanese uses words like の and もの to do this job.
They take a whole idea — a sentence, an action, a description — and turn it into something you can point to, talk about, or describe as if it were an object.

A) Phrase-following もの to imply "thing."

When following a verb phrase, adjective phrase, or noun phrase, もの functions as a nominalizer meaning "thing," "matter," "fact," or "circumstance." It turns the preceding phrase into a conceptual "thing" and often adds a reflective, explanatory, or objective tone. This usage appears frequently in written Japanese, narration, and thoughtful commentary.

Core functions:

- Turns a clause into a conceptual "thing" ("the thing that…," "the fact that…")
- Adds a conceptual or abstract sense ("such a thing as…")
- Adds reflective or narrative nuance
- Can imply circumstances or conditions surrounding an event
- Softer and more literary than koto こと when used this way

Sentence Example:
Kare wa doko de **katta** mono darou.
彼はどこで**買った**ものだろう。
I wonder where he **bought** it.

Why add mono もの to the sentence when I could just say: Doko de katta darou? Adding "mono" to a sentence in Japanese can add this subtle layer of nuance. It's kind of like saying "the thing that I bought" rather than just "what I bought." It brings a little more emphasis or helps conceptualize the event as a 'thing. So "mono" often pops up in Japanese as a way to give a bit of extra weight or a sense of tangibility to whatever you're talking about. It's almost like saying, "This is the thing that happened," rather than just "it happened."

Here, もの is the literal nominalizer meaning "thing":
買ったもの
→ "the thing (he) bought"
→ "what (he) bought"
So the structure is:

- 彼は
  he (topic)
- どこで買ったもの
  the thing he bought / what he bought
- だろう
  I wonder / probably

Put together:

彼はどこで買ったものだろう。
I wonder where he bought it

(Literally: "I wonder about the thing he bought — where was it?")

B) <u>Sentence-ending もの / もん</u>

When もの (or its softer variant もん) appears at the end of a sentence, it adds an explanatory, justifying, or reason-giving nuance. It no longer means "thing." Instead, it expresses:

- reasons
- excuses
- justifications
- emotional explanations
- "because…" with a personal tone

This usage is common in casual speech, especially when the speaker is being honest, soft, or slightly defensive.

- もの = slightly more formal, used by adults
- もん = softer, more childish, more emotional

Examples with nuance

1) Reason / justification (neutral)

<u>Ikenai</u> yo. **Shigoto** ga aru nda mono.
<u>行けない</u>よ。**仕事**があるんだもの。
I <u>can't go</u>. It's because I have **work.**
Here, もの softens the explanation — it's not cold or blunt.

2) Emotional excuse (childlike or defensive)

Datte, **shiranakatta** nda mon.
だって、**知らなかった**んだもん。
But… I **didn't know**!
This is classic "excuse-tone" Japanese — very common in speech.

3) Soft explanation of feelings

Kaeritai na. Tsukareterun da mono.
帰りたいな。疲れてるんだもの。
I **want to go home**. It's because I'm tired.
The もの makes the explanation feel personal and sincere.

> Note: Breakdown of つかれてるん (tsukareterun). It's not a single "word," but a single spoken contraction that functions as one unit.
> 1) 疲れている (tsukarete iru)
> = "am tired" (the progressive/state form of 疲れる / tsukareru = "to get tired / to become tired")
> 2) 疲れてる (tsukareteru)
> = casual contraction of 疲れている
> (いる → る)
> 3) 疲れてるの (tsukareteru no) = "it's that I'm tired"
> Here, の adds an explanatory / emotional tone.
> 4) 疲れてるん (tsukareterun)
> = contraction of 疲れてるの
> (の → ん)
> So つかれてるん literally means: "(It's that) I'm tired."

A quick comparison: mono もの vs koto こと.

- もの = concrete or conceptualized "thing" (object, event you can picture)
- こと = abstract "thing" (fact, idea, experience, rule, action)

Nan なん:

Casual contraction of なの, the noun + explanatory の construction. Adds the nuance of "the fact is…," "you see…," or "since…."
Examples:

- Gakusei nan da. 学生なんだ。I'm a student.
- Nihonjin nan dakara. 日本人なんだから。 Because I'm Japanese.
- Keisatsu nan da yo. けいさつなんだよ。(They're) the police.

"Nan" is the stem. "Da" or "Desu" is just the **copula**.
The structure is:

- なのだ → なんだ (casual explanatory)
- なのです → なんです (polite explanatory)

So:

- なん = the explanatory contraction (the stem-like unit)
- だ / です = the **copula** (casual vs. polite)

A copula is a small word that links a noun or adjective to the subject, creating an "is / am / are" relationship.
In English, the copula is the verb "to be":

- I am a student.
- She is happy.
- They are teachers.

The copula connects the subject to what it is.

Japanese doesn't use a separate verb like "to be."
Instead, it uses short endings such as:

- だ (casual)
- です (polite)

These attach to nouns and na-adjectives:

- 学生だ。= "(I) am a student."
- きれいです。= "(It) is pretty."

So in Japanese:

- だ / です = the copula
- They function like "is / am / are," but they behave more like endings than full verbs.

NOTE: "Nan" appears only after nouns and na-adjectives because they require na before the explanatory の.
Verbs and i-adjectives do not take na, so they use n instead (e.g., Iku nda, samui ndesu / 行くんだ, 寒いんです / I'm going, it's cold).
More on "ndesu んです below.

Ndesu んです:
No desu のです:

These forms belong to what linguists and textbooks usually call the Explanatory Construction, or the "Explanatory / Clarifying の (のだ・んだ)" construction.

んです / のです / なんです all come from the same structure:

[sentence] + のだ / んだ, which adds an explanatory, clarifying, or emotionally shaded nuance.

> [Note: The だ here is simply the plain-form copula—the casual equivalent of the polite です.]

They do not change the basic meaning of the sentence — they change the reason, tone, or implication. They signal that the speaker is:

- giving background
- explaining a situation
- softening a statement
- seeking clarification
- expressing emotion or personal involvement

When the の attaches to a verb or adjective, it often contracts to ん.
So:

- んです = contracted, more natural in speech/common spoken form.
- のです = Polite when used with です／ます, formal when used in writing.
- なんです = the polite explanatory form used after nouns and な-adjectives (because they require な before の). It also appears in the fixed expression Nan nan desu ka / 何なんですか / What is it, exactly?

> Note: We already covered nan なん as the stem-like contraction used after nouns and な-adjectives. Here, なんです is simply the polite explanatory expansion of that same structure.

Here are three sample sentences using んです, each showing a different nuance of the explanatory construction.

1) Giving background / explaining a situation:
Onaka ga itai n desu.
お腹が痛いんです。
I have a stomachache (that's why).
→ The speaker is explaining why they can't do something, or why they look unwell.

2) Softening a statement / adding emotional shading:
Ashita, **hayaku** okinai to ikenai n desu.
明日、早く起きないといけないんです。
I have to get up **early** tomorrow, you see.
→ Adds gentle explanation rather than a blunt statement.

The literal structure is:
Tomorrow, if I don't wake up early, it won't do, you see.
The Japanese expresses it through a *negative conditional obligation*:

- **起きないといけない。**
  "If I don't wake up, it won't be acceptable" → "I must wake up."

And the **んです** adds: explanation, background, softening, or emotional shading.

So the speaker is gently explaining why they can't stay out late, or why they're going home, or why they're tired. The obligation itself is expressed in Japanese through a double-negative pattern (起きないといけない).

NOTE: Japanese can express obligation in a positive structure, but it sounds formal or unnatural in everyday conversation because the language has no direct equivalent of "must." So Japanese uses a double-negative pattern because that's the native way the language encodes obligation.

English has a direct, positive verb meaning:
- "I must ___."
- "I have to ___."

Japanese does not have a single, positive verb that means "must." So instead, Japanese expresses obligation through a logical structure:
"If I don't do X, it won't be acceptable."
→ therefore, I must do X.
It's not "double negative for style." It's "double negative because that's how Japanese encodes necessity."

3) Seeking clarification / asking for the reason

Dōshite konakatta n desu ka.
どうして来なかったんですか。
Why didn't you come?
→ The んですか demands an explanation or expresses strong emotion. Depending on tone, it can signal genuine concern ("Oh no, why couldn't you make it?") or sound accusatory ("Why didn't you come?").

Pronunciation Note: In natural Japanese speech, the i in shi often becomes light, shortened, or slightly devoiced when followed by another consonant. This is the same pattern you've already seen in:
- shita → sh'ta
- shite → sh'te

- suki → ski

Because shi + te blends quickly, the i becomes very soft, almost whispered.
What learners often hear: dosh'te
What's actually happening: The i is still there — just reduced due to natural vowel devoicing.

Here are three sample sentences using のです, slightly more formal / written.

1) Giving background / explaining.

Kare wa **byōki** na no desu.
彼は**病気**なのです。
He is **sick** (that's the reason).
→ Supplies background information that explains something the listener already noticed or wondered about. Without のです, it would simply be:

Kare wa byōki desu.
彼は病気です。
He is sick. (neutral fact)

2) Softening / clarifying in writing.

Watashi wa **hajimete** kita no desu.
私は**初めて**来たのです。
This is my **first time** coming.
→ Here, のです softens the statement and adds a gentle self-disclosure tone. It implies:

- "I'm explaining why I might seem unsure or unfamiliar."
- "Please understand my situation."

It's often used when someone wants to politely frame their inexperience without sounding abrupt or blunt. Without のです:

Watashi wa **hajimete** kimashita.
私は**初めて**来ました。
I came for the **first time**. (simple statement)

3) Seeking clarification (intense or highly focused tone).

Sono **imi** wa nan na no desu ka.
その**意味**は何なのですか。
What on earth does that **mean**?

→ Adding なのですか to a question word like "what" (nan) actually amplifies the question. It demands an explanation and can easily sound intense, confrontational, or deeply perplexed. It implies:

- "I am demanding or urgently needing an explanation."
- "Just what exactly is the meaning behind that?"

Compared to:

Sono imi wa nan desu ka.
その意味は何ですか。
What does that mean? (neutral)
Adding のです softens the question and adds a sense of:
I'm asking because I need clarification — please elaborate.

Here are three example sentences using なんです — after nouns / な-adjectives, or "what is it?"

1) After a noun

Ashita wa **shiken** nan desu.
明日は**試験**なんです。
I have an **exam** tomorrow.

Learners are quick to ask, "Why not say 持っている (motte iru) for "I have"? Or, "Why not say あります (arimasu) for "there is"?

A) Motte iru 持っている means "to physically possess something." Motsu 持つ (verb) / 持っている is used for objects you can hold, own, or carry.

- 本を持っている — I have a book
- 傘を持っている — I have an umbrella
- お金を持っている — I have money

But you cannot "hold" or "possess" an exam in that sense. An exam is an event, not an object.
So:
Ashita wa shiken o motte iru.
明日は試験を持っている。
sounds like "I am physically holding an exam," which is incorrect.

B) Arimasu あります means "there exists," not "I have an event." ある / あります is used for:

- objects existing somewhere
- events happening somewhere
- things that "are" in a location

So you can say:

Ashita wa shiken ga arimasu.
明日は試験があります。
There is an exam tomorrow.
This is perfectly correct Japanese.

But it's not the same nuance as:
Ashita wa shiken nan desu.
明日は試験なんです。
I have an exam tomorrow (and that's why…).

2) After a な-adjective

Kono **heya** wa shizuka na ndesu.
この**部屋**は静かなんです。
This **room** is quiet, you see.

3) Asking "what is it?" / seeking explanation

Nan nan desu ka, sore wa.
何なんですか、それは。
What is that, exactly?

Sidebar: 何ですか vs. 何なんですか (Nan desu ka vs. Nan nan desu ka)

何ですか (Nan desu ka)
Plain "What is it?"

- Neutral
- Direct
- Used to identify an object or ask for basic information
- No explanatory nuance

Example:
Kore wa nan desu ka.
これは何ですか。
What is this?

This is simply nan + desu + ka.
It does not use the explanatory んです structure.

何なんですか (Nan nan desu ka)
"What is this (really)?" / "What's going on?"

- Requests explanation or background
- Softer, more emotional
- Can express confusion, frustration, curiosity, or "Tell me the story behind this"

Example:
Nan nan desu ka, sore.
何なんですか、それ。
What is that supposed to be?
What's going on with that?

This does use the explanatory structure:
nan + n + desu + ka → なんですか

Key Difference (One Line for Learners)

- 何ですか = plain "What is it?"
- 何なんですか = "What is it (really)?" with explanatory nuance

End Sidebar

No の:

A particle with several major functions. Beginners first learn it as a possessive marker, but in explanatory and causal contexts, の acts as a nominalizer and as a sentence-ending particle that adds soft explanation, background, or emotional tone. The possessive の and the classifier の ("the one") are separate functions and do not express explanation or cause.

1) Nominalizer の (turning clauses into "noun-like units").

The particle の attaches to an entire clause and turns it into a noun-like unit so that particles such as を, は, or が can attach to it. **Japanese cannot attach particles directly to a raw verb or clause**, so の is required to make the clause grammatically usable.

Here is a clean, logical progression:

1. の turns a verb clause into a noun-like unit.
2. Only noun-like units can take particles.
3. Therefore, 君が来る (kimi ga kuru) needs の before を.
4. That's why 君が来るのを待っていた (Kimi ga kuru no o matte ita) is grammatical.
5. And why 君が来るを待っていた (Kimi ga kuru o matte ita) is impossible.

This の is similar to こと, but:

- koto こと is neutral, factual, abstract
- no の is personal, concrete, emotional, or sensory

Examples:
Kimi ga kuru no o matte ita.
君が来るのを待っていた。
I was waiting for **you** to come.
(literally: "I was waiting for the object of you to come.")

Ame ga furu no ga **kikoeru**.
雨が降るのが**聞こえる**。
I **can hear** the rain falling.
(literally: "I can hear the sound of rain falling.")

> Note: Kikoeru 聞こえる is a full verb. More specifically, it belongs to a special class of intransitive perception verbs. It is not derived from the verb kiku 聞く (listen). It's not a conjugation. It's not a potential form. It's not "聞く + える." It is its own independent verb with its own dictionary entry and its own meaning: 聞こえる = to be audible / to be heard naturally. This is why, for beginners, the える ending is misleading. It looks like a potential form, but it isn't one.

Neko ga **hashiru** no o mita.
猫が**走る**のを見た。
I saw the cat **run**.

2) Explanatory の (sentence-ending の).
When の appears at the end of a sentence (often with da / だ or desu / です omitted), it adds:
- explanation
- softening
- emotional tone
- seeking understanding

It is the plain-form equivalent of ndesu んです / no desu のです.

Dōshite **konakatta** no?
どうして**来なかった**の？
Why **didn't you come**?
(soft, seeking explanation)

Ima **dekakeru** no.
今**出かける**の。
I'm **heading out** now.
(explaining your situation)

Samui no.
寒いの。
I'm **cold**.
(giving background, soft tone)

Sore wa **chigau** no.
それは**違う**の。
That's **not right**.
(soft correction)

> Note: What chigau ちがう actually means. Learners often memorize it as "to be wrong," but its core meaning is: to differ / to be different. From that meaning, the "wrong" sense naturally emerges:
> - If something "differs" from what is correct → it's wrong.
> - If someone's assumption "differs" from reality → they're mistaken.

Sentence-ending の adds a gentle explanatory tone, especially in:
- women's speech
- children's speech
- soft, emotional, or intimate contexts
- situations where you want understanding rather than confrontation

Men often use nda んだ / nda yo んだよ instead, but の is not exclusive to women, it's just softer.

Nuance comparison:
- の nominalizes sensory, emotional, or personal experiences.
- こと nominalizes facts, rules, general truths.

Node ので:

A conjunction meaning "because / since / as." It connects a reason to a result, but with a softer, more polite, more objective tone than kara から.

> Politeness & Softness Compared to から
> - から = direct, personal, sometimes blunt
> - ので = gentle, explanatory, polite
>
> Example difference:
> - Ikenai kara – 行けないから。 → "I can't go (because…)."
> - Ikenai node – 行けないので。 → "Since I can't go…" (softer)

Node Usage Examples:
Ame na node, dekakemasen.
雨なので、出かけません。
Since it's raining, I won't go out.

The な appears because ので requires the explanatory の, and nouns need な to connect to の:

- Ame 雨 (rain) → 雨なので
- Benri 便利 (convenience) → 便利なので
- Gakusei 学生 (student) → 学生なので

Nouns do NOT "take な" by themselves. They only take な when followed by のです / ので / なら / なので, etc.

Isogashii node, ikemasen.
忙しいので、行けません。
Because I'm busy, I can't go.

Minna sorotta node, itadakimasu.
みんなそろったので、いただきます。
Since everyone is here, let's eat.

Why the "no" の in "node" is there:
The の before で is actually the explanatory の, which turns the clause into a noun-like phrase.
Think of it as:

- "the fact that…"
- "the situation is that…"

So:

- Isogashī node – 忙しいので

literally = "because the situation is that I'm busy"
This makes the tone softer, more polite, less blunt, and more "reason-based" rather than emotional.

Noni のに:

A conjunctive particle with the core meaning: "even though…," "despite the fact that…," "although…" Emotional tone: frustration, disappointment, surprise, regret, or contradiction.

のに connects two clauses where the first clause gives a reason or condition, but the second clause contradicts what should logically follow. This creates a sense of "this should not have happened" or "I expected something else." It is one of the strongest contrastive connectors in Japanese, often carrying emotional weight.

1) Basic contradiction ("even though…"). The speaker states a fact, then expresses a result that shouldn't logically follow.

Ame ga futte iru noni, kare wa dekaketa.
雨が降っているのに、彼は出かけた。
He went out even though it's raining.

Kantan na mondai na noni, machigaeta.
簡単な問題なのに、間違えた。
I got it wrong even though it was an **easy** question.
Nuance: surprise, contradiction, mild frustration.

2) Emotional complaint ("and yet…!" / "but why…?") When spoken with emotion, のに becomes a soft complaint or lament. This is extremely common in conversation and fiction.

Ganbatta noni…
頑張ったのに...
I **worked so hard**, and yet…

Zenbu tsukutta noni, daremo tabenai.
全部作ったのに、誰も食べない。
I made **all** this (food), and nobody's eating it.
Nuance: hurt feelings, disappointment, emotional contradiction.

> Note: In fast, natural speech, tsukutta may sound like ts'kutta because the u in tsu weakens between voiceless consonants. The vowel is still present, just reduced.
>
> Note: daremo だれも is one word. In negative sentences, it means "nobody" or "no one." In affirmative sentences, daremo usually means "anyone," though the affirmative use is less common in everyday speech.

3) Positive expectation violated ("I thought…" / "I expected…") Here のに expresses a mismatch between expectation and reality.

Kuru to omotta noni, **konakatta**.
来ると思ったのに、**来なかった**。
I thought he would come, but he **didn't (come)**.

Atsui noni, **daremo** mizu o nomanai.
暑いのに、**誰も**水を飲まない。
It's hot, yet **nobody** is drinking water.

Nuance: surprise or confusion.

4) Gentle reproach ("you should…" / "why didn't you…?") When used toward another person, のに can sound like a gentle scolding.

Hayaku ieba yokatta noni.
早く言えばよかったのに。
You should have told me earlier.

> Note: 言えば (ieba) is the "if" conditional form of 言う (iu) = "to say."
> 言えば = "if (you) say / if (you) had said"
>
> Note: Yokatta よかった is the past tense of いい (good), but in this construction it means: "it would have been good if…" "I wish you had…" This is the classic regret pattern: 〜ばよかった (〜ba yokatta) = "should have…" / "I wish (you/I) had…"

Mō **sukoshi** matte kurereba ii noni.
もう**少し**待ってくれればいいのに。
You could have waited **a little** longer.

> Note: the "u" in すこし / 少し (sukoshi) is often devoiced between s and k, making it sound like s'koshi in natural speech. The vowel is still present, just weakened.

Nuance: soft criticism, mild reproach, regret on behalf of the listener.

5) Noni のに with nouns and na-adjectives. のに requires the explanatory な before nouns and na-adjectives.

Kirei na noni, **ninki** ga nai.
綺麗なのに、**人気**がない。
It's beautiful, yet it's not **popular**.

Gakusei na noni, **okane** ga aru.
学生なのに、**お金**がある。
He's a student, yet he has **money.**

Shi し:

This is the listing / reason-giving connector and is much richer than most textbooks admit. Learners love this particle once they see how flexible it is. It means: "and besides" / plus the fact that / because. It also adds a reason that leads into the next clause. Here are some major functions of し.

1. Listing reasons:

Saikin wa **kankōkyaku** mō ooi shi, tsukareru ndesu yo ne.
最近は**観光客**もう多いし、疲れるんですよね。
There are so many **tourists** these days, and it's getting tiring, you know?

Shi can also be used in multiple reasons, often with a soft, emotional tone.
For example:

Atsui shi, nemui shi, kyō wa **dekaketakunai.**
暑いし、眠いし、今日は**出かけたくない**。
It's hot, I'm sleepy, and **I don't want to go out** today.

> Note: Dekaketakunai 出かけたくない looks long, but it's built from a very regular pattern.
> To express "want to do X", Japanese attaches たい (tai) to the verb stem:
> - 出かける → 出かけたい
>   "to go out" → "want to go out"
>
> To make this desire negative ("don't want to"), Japanese treats たい like an i-adjective.
> That means you can apply the normal i-adjective negative ending:
> たい → たくない
>
> Here's the step-by-step:
>
> a) Take the verb stem:
> 出かける → 出かけ (stem: 出かけ)
>
> b) Add たい to express desire:
> 出かけ たい = "want to go out"
>
> c) Drop the final い of たい and attach くない, just like any i-adjective:
> たい → たくない

d) Result:
出かけたくない = "don't want to go out"

So in the sentence:
暑いし、眠いし、今日は出かけたくない。
It's hot, I'm sleepy, and I don't want to go out today.

The し is linking multiple reasons, and 出かけたくない expresses a negative desire formed through the regular たい → たくない adjective pattern.

Saikin isogashī shi, **okane** mo naishi…
最近忙しいし、**お金**もないし…
I've been busy lately, and I don't have **money** either…

2. Listing qualities (not reasons). This is a different nuance: piling up positive or negative traits.

Kono mise wa yasui shi, oishī shi, **saikō** da yo.
この店は安いし、美味しいし、**最高**だよ。
This place is cheap, tasty, and just **great.**

Note: In the above example, da だ is the plain form of the polite desu です.

Kare wa yasashī shi, **yoku** ki ga tsuku shi…
彼は優しいし、**よく**気がつくし…
He's kind, and he's **really** attentive…

Note: In "kigatsuku" the first "u" weakens so much in natural speech that it can sound like it disappears. The whole thing blends into something like "ki-ga-ts'ku"

Note: Here, し is not causal, it's additive. It creates a warm, enthusiastic tone and is great for describing people, places, and opinions.

3. Softening statements / avoiding directness. Japanese speakers often use し to avoid sounding too blunt.

Ikitakunai shi…
行きたくないし…
I mean… I don't really want to go, you know…

Kyō wa chotto isogashī shi…
今日はちょっと忙しいし…
I'm kind of busy today, so…

This is the "trailing off" し — it implies a reason without fully stating it.

4. Creating a "justification tone" (defensive or explanatory). When someone is explaining themselves, し adds a soft justification.

Examples:
Datte, shiranakatta shi!
だって、知らなかったし！
Well, I didn't know, okay?

Muri da yo. **Jikan** nai shi.
無理だよ。**時間**ないし。
I can't. I don't have **time**.

> Note: Muri da you 無理だよ can mean "I can't," "It's impossible," or "That's too much for me."

This is not listing multiple reasons — it's strengthening a single reason by giving it emotional weight. Very natural in spoken Japanese.

5. し at the end of a sentence (unfinished, emotional). This is a very common conversational pattern.

Kyō wa **tsukareta** shi…
今日は**疲れた**し…
I'm **tired** today, so… (implying: "don't expect much from me")

Betsu ni īshi.
別にいいし。
Whatever, it's fine. (slightly defensive)

> Note: Betsuni 別に means: not really; not particularly; it's nothing (special); I don't especially care. It is used to downplay, dismiss, or show indifference toward something. Betsuni often appears with a negative verb or in casual speech where the negative is implied.
> Nuance:
> - soft indifference

- mild dismissal
- "it's nothing" / "I don't mind" / "I don't care that much"

Examples:

- Betsuni ī yo. → It's fine, whatever.
- Betsuni suki ja nai. → I don't particularly like it.
- Betsuni… → Not really… (trailing off)

Ikanakute mo īshi.
行かなくてもいいし。
You don't have to go anyway.

Sentence-final し often implies "I could say more, but I won't." It's one of the most expressive uses. It shows how Japanese expresses emotion through incompleteness.

6. し in polite speech (ですし / ますし). Yes — し attaches to polite forms too. It is not casual-only.

Ame desushi, samui desushi, kyō wa yamemashou.
雨ですし、寒いですし、今日はやめましょう。
It's raining, and it's cold, so let's skip it today.

Jikan mo arimasenshi, koko made ni shimasu.
時間もありませんし、ここまでにします。
We're out of time, so let's stop here.

7. し used to "pad" a statement (softening opinions). This is subtle but very natural.

Mā, ī n janai desu ka. Yasui desushi.
まあ、いいんじゃないですか。安いですし。
Well, I think it's fine. It's cheap, after all.

Kare, yasashī desushi, ī hito desu yo.
彼、優しいですし、いい人ですよ。
He's kind, and he's a good person.

Here し adds a gentle, supportive tone.

Shite して:

This word is the te-form of the verb suru する(to do). In Japanese, many nouns can become verbs simply by attaching する (to do) to them. These are called suru-verbs or verbal nouns. So when you take a noun like:

- benkyou - 勉強 → "study"
  → 勉強する = "to study"
- undou - 運動 → "exercise"
  → 運動する = "to exercise"
- anshin - 安心 → "peace of mind"
  → 安心する = "to feel at ease / to be relieved"

More examples:

NOUN	+する	MEANING
setsumei	説明する	to explain
unten	運転する	to drive
renshuu	練習する	to practice
kansha	感謝する	to express gratitude

And then:

- Kansha shite iimashita - 感謝して言いました = (He) said it with gratitude
- Renshū shite **jōzu** ni natta - 練習して**上手**になった = (I) practiced and **got better**

When do I need the shite-form?

して is the "connector" form of する.

When a する - verb (like anshin suru 安心する, renshū suru 練習する, benkyō suru 勉強する) is followed by another action or when it describes the manner or background state of another action, it changes to して.

1. Connecting actions
   - **Benkyō** shite nemasu.
   - **勉強**して寝ます。
   - I'll **study** and then sleep.

2. Describing the manner of an action
   - **Anshin** shite taberaremasu.
   - **安心**して食べられます。
   - I can eat with **peace of mind.**

3. Requests: して is used because kudasai ください attaches to the connector form of the verb.
   - **Setsumei** shite kudasai.
   - **説明**してください。
   - Please **explain.**

4. Progressive form: している literally means "doing (it) now."
- Benkyō shite iru.
- 勉強している。
- I'm studying.

If a suru-verb is not the final verb in the sentence, it almost always becomes して. When it links two actions, it often feels like "and" in English. **But it's important to note that して is not fundamentally the word "and."**

Examples:
- **Ryokō** shite shashin o totta.
  旅行して写真を撮った。
  I **traveled** and took photos.

- **Renshū** shite jōzu ni natta
  練習して上手になった。
  I **practiced** and got better.

- **Kansha** shite iimashita.
  感謝して言いました。
  He spoke with **gratitude**.

Wake わけ:

Japanese usually writes the grammatical わけ in kana. It is a noun with the core meaning: **reason, logic, grounds, the conclusion that follows**. It is unrelated to the word 訳 (wake) meaning "translation" or "meaning," even though they share the same pronunciation.

In grammar, わけ expresses the reasoning behind something, the logic that connects cause and effect, or the conclusion that naturally follows from a situation. It often appears in set patterns that express justification, inevitability, or emphatic contradiction.

1) Logical conclusion ("so that means…"). わけだ shows that something is the natural or logical result of what came before.

Atsui wake da.
暑いわけだ。
No wonder it's hot. / So that's why it's hot.

Kare wa nihon ni **sunde ita**. Nihongo ga umai wake da.
彼は日本に**住んでいた**。日本語がうまいわけだ。
He **lived** in Japan. So of course his Japanese is good.

Nuance: explanation, realization, "ah, that makes sense."

> Note: 住んで (sunde) comes from 住む (sumu) = "to live / reside." Like many verbs of existence or placement, 住む uses に to mark the location: 東京に住んでいる = "I live in Tokyo." The te-form 住んで appears in expressions like 住んでいる ("am living") and 住んでいた ("used to live").

1) Justification / reason ("the reason is…"). わけ can explicitly present the reason behind something.

Sonna wake ja nai.
そんなわけじゃない。
That's not the reason. / It's not like that.

Okurenakya naranai wake ga atta.
遅れなきゃならないわけがあった。
There was a reason I had to be late.
Nuance: clarifying motives, giving justification.

> Note: 遅れなきゃ (okurenakya) is the contracted form of 遅れなければ (okurenakereba), the negative conditional of 遅れる (okureru) meaning "to be late." Okurenakya means "if (someone) isn't late" or "if (someone) doesn't get delayed." In the pattern 遅れなきゃならない (okurenakya naranai), the meaning becomes "must be late" because the negative conditional (なきゃ) attaches to the verb, and ならない supplies the "must" meaning.
> Follow the contraction:
> - 遅れる (okureru) → base verb
> - 遅れない (okurenai) → negative form
> - 遅れなければ (okurenakereba) → negative conditional ("if not late"). It is polite, careful, or neutral speech.
> - 遅れなきゃ (okurenakya) → contracted conversational form. It is casual and very common
>
> **Both okurenakya and okurenakereba can be used in speech depending on formality.**

Note: ならない (naranai) is the negative of なる = to become. But in the grammar pattern:
～なきゃならない (～nakya naranai)
the ならない does NOT mean "does not become." Instead, it is part of a fixed expression meaning: **must / have to.** So:

- 行かなきゃならない (Ikanakya naranai) = I must go
- 食べなきゃならない (Tabenakya naranai) = I must eat
- 遅れなきゃならない (Okurenakya naranai) = I must be late

2) Strong denial ("there's no way…!"). わけがない is one of the strongest ways to say something is impossible or unthinkable.

Kare ga **makeru** wake ga nai.
彼が**負ける**わけがない。
There's no way he would **lose**.

Sonna koto aru wake nai yo.
そんなことあるわけないよ。
There's no way that could happen.
Nuance: emphatic contradiction, certainty.

3) "It doesn't mean that…" (わけではない / わけじゃない). This softens or partially denies an assumption.

Kirai na wake ja nai.
嫌いなわけじゃない。
It's not that I **dislike** it.

Hima na wake de wa nai.
暇なわけではない。
It's not that I'm **free** (I'm actually busy).

Nuance: partial denial, clarification, nuance-adjustment.

4) "That's why…" / "So that's the reason…" (wake de / わけで). Cause and effect are connected mid-sentence.

Ame datta wake de, ikenakatta.
雨だったわけで、行けなかった。
Since it was **raining**, that's why I couldn't go.
Nuance: explanatory connection.

5) “In other words…” / “That is to say…” (to iu wake de / というわけで). A natural transition used in speech and writing.

To iu wake de, kyou wa **owari** ni shimasu.
というわけで、今日は**終わり**にします。
And with that, we’ll **wrap up** for today.

Nuance: summarizing, transitioning, concluding.

PART V: EXCESS & COMBINATION

Key stems and nuances in this section:

- ～ba ～ば, ～nara ～なら, ～tara ～たら, → Conditional forms
- ～ba ī ～ばいい / ～tara ī ～たらいい → Suggestion/hope
- ～chatta ～ちゃった → Adds psychological commentary on the verb
- ～gatera ～がてら → "While doing / on the occasion of"
- ～gatte ～がって → Expressing others' feelings/desires
- ～nakute ～なくて → Negative conjunctive
- ～sō そう → "about to," "on the verge of," imminent action
- demo でも → Unexpectedness, inclusion, or contrast
- gurai ぐらい / kurai くらい → Approximation
- made まで → Limit ("until / up to"); also "even" in contexts of unexpected inclusion. In this category, it is treated as a particle attaching to nouns, verbs, or time expressions, not entire clauses.)
- mo も→ an intensifier of degree (even/not even, also, as well)
- shika nai しかない → Restrictive "nothing but"
- sugiru すぎる → Excess ("too much")
- to と → particle for combination / listing / "and / with"

Vocabulary to review:

ane	姉	older sister
ani	兄	older brother
atarashii	新しい	new
bijutsukan	美術館	art museum
densha	電車	electric train (does not include diesel, steam or Shinkansen)
furu	降る	to fall (rain, snow, etc.)
genki	元気	healthy, energetic, lively, well, fine (in health or spirit)
hare	晴れ	sunny
hazukashī	恥ずかしい	embarrassing
hiraku	開く	to open, to unfold, to spread, to hold (an event)
hitsuyō	必要	necessary, need
hōhō	方法 (ほうほう)	method, way, means, manner of doing something
hotondo	ほとんど	almost all, most, nearly

ippai	いっぱい	full, filled up, a full amount, a lot, plenty, to the brim / super, really (in speech) / as a counter
isogu	急ぐ	to hurry
kaimono	買い物	shopping
kanojo	彼女	she
kasa	傘	umbrella
kōen	公園	park
kutsu	靴	shoes
moshi	もし	what if, suppose, in case, let's imagine that
naku	泣く	to cry, to weep
nebō	寝坊	oversleeping
osu	押す	push
otosu	落とす	to drop (something)
renraku	連絡	contact, communication
saku	咲く	bloom
sakura	桜	cherry blossoms
sanpo	散歩	walk, stroll
shinpai	心配	anxiety, worry
shinu	死ぬ	to die
sōdan	相談	consultation
suberu	滑る	to slip, slide, glide, fail, or fall flat
sugu	すぐ	immediately
suku	空く	to become empty (When referring to the stomach – to get hungry)
takushī	タクシー	taxi
tegami	手紙	letter
wasureru	忘れる	to forget
yasui	やすい (易い)	easy to do / likely to happen (inexpensive when using the kanji 安)
yasumu	休む	to rest, take time off, retire for the night, to pause
yoru	寄る	to stop by, to approach, to come near / (also evening using a different kanji)

Diving further into the stems and nuances

～ba ～ば:

Conditional Stem Core (Hypothetical / Natural Result / General Truth). It means "if / when," expressing a natural, logical, or expected result. ～ば is the most neutral, least emotional of the Japanese conditionals. It describes:

- general truths
- natural consequences
- logical outcomes
- hypothetical conditions
- non-volitional results (things that happen naturally, not by intention)

It is not typically used for commands, requests, or volitional actions by the speaker. It expresses a condition that naturally leads to a result. The result feels like the "obvious" or "expected" outcome. This is why ～ば often appears in explanations, advice, general statements, and hypothetical reasoning.

Formation:
Verbs

- taberu 食べる → tabereba 食べれば (if you eat it)
- iku 行く → ikeba 行けば (if you go)
- suru する → sureba すれば (if you do)
- kuru 来る → kureba 来れば (if you come)

Adjectives

- takai 高い → takakereba 高ければ (if it's expensive)
- samui 寒い → samukereba 寒ければ (if it's cold)
- benri da 便利だ → benri nara 便利なら → benri naraba 便利ならば (if it's convenient)
- shizuka da 静かだ → shizuka nara 静かなら → shizuka naraba 静かならば

Nouns

- yasumi 休み → yasuminaraba 休みならば (if it's a holiday)
- Nihonjin 日本人 → Nihonjin-naraba 日本人ならば (if you are Japanese)

Note: ならば is more formal/emphatic than なら.

1) Natural consequence (A → naturally leads to → B). This is the most common use.

Ame ga fureba, <u>michi</u> ga **suberi** yasuku naru.
雨が降れば、<u>道</u>が**滑り**やすくなる。
If it rains, the <u>roads</u> become **slippery**.
No emotion, no intention, just a natural result.

Note: Yasuku やすく is the adverbial form of the adjective yasui やすい, which attaches to verbs to mean "easy to do." When やすい is attached to a verb stem, it means: easy to do / likely to happen. Examples:

- tabe yasui 食べやすい = easy to eat
- koware yasui 壊れやすい = easy to break
- wasure yasui 忘れやすい = easy to forget

So:
suberi yasuku naru 滑りやすくなる
= 滑りやすい (easy to slip)

- ku (く) makes yasui adverbial
- なる (to become)

→ "to become slippery / to become easy to slip."

2) General truths / universal statements. Used like "when X happens, Y is generally true."

<u>Haru</u> ni nareba, **atatakaku** naru.
<u>春</u>になれば、**暖かく**なる。
When <u>spring</u> comes, it gets **warm**.

Note: なれば (nareba) is simply the "if / when" form of the verb なる (naru), which means "to become." It combines the idea of change (なる = become) with the conditional ば ("if / when"), giving you a smooth, neutral way to say:

- "if it becomes warm" → atatakaku nareba あたたかくなれば
- "if it becomes quiet" → shizuka ni nareba しずかになれば
- "if it becomes necessary" → hitsuyō ni nareba ひつようになれば

3) Hypothetical reasoning ("if it were the case…"). Used for imagining a situation.

Okane ga <u>areba</u>, **ryokō** shitai.
お金が<u>あれば</u>、**旅行**したい。
<u>If I had</u> money, I'd like to **travel**.
This is not a request or command, just a hypothetical.

Note: あれば (areba) is one of those forms that feels like "if I had," but the nuance depends on what comes before it. あれば = "if there is / if it exists / if I have / if you have." So yes, あれば can mean "if I had," but only when the context is possession.

4) Advice stated as a natural consequence. Not a command, more like "if you do X, good things happen."

Hayaku nereba, genki ni narimasu yo.
早く寝れば、元気になりますよ。
If you sleep **early**, you'll feel better.
This is softer and more neutral than ～たら.

5) Polite or formal reasoning (ならば). It adds weight or formality.

Hitsuyō de areba, itsudemo taiō itashimasu.
必要であれば、いつでも対応いたします。
If it's **necessary**, we will handle it at any time.

Sidebar: What ～ba (～ば) does not do

1) Not used for direct commands.
Ame ga fureba, **kasa** o motte itte.
雨が降れば、**傘**を持って行って。
If it rains, take an **umbrella** with you.
Sounds unnatural. Use ～tara (～たら) instead.

Note: As we discussed, ～ば is not natural for giving commands, because ～ば expresses a neutral, natural consequence, not a volitional instruction. So the correct ～たら version is:

Ame ga futtara, kasa o motte itte.
雨が降ったら、傘を持って行って。
If it rains, take an umbrella.
This is the natural, conversational, and correct way to express a conditional + command.

Note: もっていって (motte itte) comes from two verbs working together:

- 持つ (motsu) — to hold / to have / to carry
- 行く (iku) — to go

When combined as 持って行って (motte itte), the meaning becomes: "take it with you." Literally: "have it / carry it, and go." Japanese often links verbs like this to show a sequence of actions that form one natural idea. So 持って行く doesn't feel like two separate steps, it's simply the everyday way to say "take (something) along."

2) Not used for speaker's intentional actions.

Jikan ga areba, ikimasu.
時間があれば、行きます。
If I have time, I'll go.

It's not wrong, but it sounds stiff and is not the natural choice for everyday conversation. In real speech, people naturally say:

Jikan ga attara, ikimasu.
時間があったら、行きます。
If I have time, I'll go.

3) Not used for invitations.
Hima ga areba, kite kudasai.
暇があれば、来てください。
If you have some **free time**, please come (and visit).
Sounds stiff. It's better when said:
Hima dattara, kite kudasai.
暇だったら、来てください。
If you have some free time, please come (and visit).

End Sidebar

Comparison Box: 〜ば vs. 〜たら vs. 〜なら vs. と:

Form	Core Meaning	Personality / Nuance	Natural Uses	Example
〜ば	If/when (logical result)	Neutral, logical, natural consequence. No emotion.	General truths, natural outcomes, hypothetical reasoning, explanations.	雨が降れば、寒くなる。If it rains, it gets cold.
〜たら	If/when (after X happens)	Event-based, real-life, practical. "After X, then Y."	Everyday decisions, commands, requests, invitations, speaker intention.	雨が降ったら、傘を持って行って。If it rains, take an umbrella.
〜なら	If it's true that / If it's the case that	Assumption-based, topic-setting. Responds to information.	Giving advice based on what the listener said; conditional suggestions; "if it's about X…"	雨なら、家にいよう。If it's raining (as you say), let's stay home.
〜と	When / whenever	Automatic, inevitable, cause-	Natural laws, habitual results,	雨が降ると、道が滑る。When it

		and-effect. No control.	machine-like outcomes.	rains, the roads get slippery.

Note: Many verbs produce the form ～えば when conjugated into the ～ば conditional (e.g., aeba 会えば — "if we meet," ieba 言えば — "if you say so," omoeba 思えば — "if you think about it"). This is not a separate grammar pattern, just the natural result of the ～ば formation rules.

～ba ii ～ばいい:

Suggestion / "Should / Ought to / It would be good if…" Even though it contains ～ば, this expression does not behave like the neutral, logical ～ば you just covered. ～ばいい is an idiomatic pattern used for giving advice, offering solutions, or asking what someone should do. The literal structure is "if you do X, it will be good," but in real Japanese it simply means:

- "You should do X."
- "Why don't you do X?"
- "What should I do?" (in question form)

This pattern is extremely common in everyday conversation. Example sentences:

1) Advice / suggestion
Motto nereba ii yo.
もっと寝ればいいよ。
You should sleep more.

2) Offering a solution
Wakaranakereba, **kikeba ii**.
わからなければ、**聞けばいい。**
If you don't understand, **you should ask**.

3) Asking what someone should do
Dō sureba ii desu ka.
どうすればいいですか。
What should I do?
This one is extremely common.

4) Soft reassurance
Ki ni shinakereba ii yo.
気にしなければいいよ。
You don't need to worry about it.

Note: しなければ (shinakereba) is the ～なければ (negative-conditional) form of the verb:

- する (suru) — to do
- しない (shinai) — not do
- しなければ (shinakereba) — if (someone) doesn't do

So by itself, しなければ simply means: "if you don't do (it)." It's only when paired with 気 (ki) in the expression ki ni suru (気にする) that it gains the meaning:

- ki ni shinai 気にしない — not worry / not care / to not mind
- ki ni shinakereba 気にしなければ — if you don't worry about it

The meaning comes from the idiom 気にする, not from しなければ alone. (気にする was covered in Part IV: Explanatory & Causal.)

～chatta ～ちゃった:

This stem is the contracted form of ～てしまった (te shimatta). The pattern ～てしまった expresses unintended actions, regret, accidents, or emotionally marked completion; things like "ended up doing…," "accidentally did…," or "oops, I did…."

So ～ちゃった adds psychological commentary to the verb. It tells the listener how the speaker feels about the action.

1) Unintentional action:

Zenbu tabechatta.
全部食べちゃった。
I ended up eating **all of it**.

2) Regret / "Oops…":

Nebō shichatta.
寝坊しちゃった。
Oops, I **overslept**.

3) Mild apology:

Gomen, **wasurechatta**.
ごめん、**忘れちゃった**。
Sorry, **I forgot**.

4) Emotional completion:

Kono hon, mō **yonjatta** yo.
この本、もう読んじゃったよ。
I already **finished reading** this book.

Side-note: Why is it yonjatta and not yonchatta? The verb 読む (yomu) forms its 〜て-form as: 読んで (yonde), not yomute or yomite. This is because 読む is a godan -mu verb, and all -mu verbs form their 〜て-form with 〜んで.

So when you attach 〜でしまった → 〜じゃった, the contraction follows the same rule:

1. 読む
2. 読んでしまった (yonde shimatta) — "ended up reading"
3. 読んじゃった (yonjatta) — contracted form

The んで → んじゃった contraction is automatic.

There is no point in the conjugation where a "cha" sound appears, because:

- ちゃった comes from 〜てしまった
- じゃった comes from 〜でしまった

Since 読む uses 〜んで, not 〜んて, the correct contraction is: 読んじゃった (yonjatta), not yonchatta.

This is the same pattern seen in:
• nomu 飲む → 飲んで → nonjatta 飲んじゃった (I drank it)
• shinu 死ぬ → 死んで → shin jatta 死んじゃった (Someone died)
• asobu 遊ぶ → 遊んで → ason jatta 遊んじゃった (I played around)
The "ja" comes from でしまった, not from the verb itself.

5) Accident:

Saifu o otoshichatta.
財布を落としちゃった。
I accidentally dropped my **wallet**.

〜chattari (〜ちゃったり):

A verb conjugation pattern meaning "ended up doing (among other things)." It comes from the contraction of ～てしまう ("to end up doing") combined with the ～たり listing form.

Example formation (hanasu = to talk):
話す → 話してしまう → 話しちゃう → 話しちゃった → 話しちゃったり

This pattern expresses an action that someone ended up doing, **listed as one item among several possible actions.**

Examples:
Hanashichattari suru - 話しちゃったりする - I end up talking (among other things).

> Note: In casual speech, the "shi" in forms like 話しちゃったり often softens or blends into the following "cha," making it sound like "hanachattari." This is a natural vowel reduction in spoken Japanese and does not change the meaning.
>
> It's the same reason:
> - したくない sounds like sh'takunai
> - している sounds like sh'teru
> - どうして sounds like doush'te

Tabechattari shita - 食べちゃったりした - I ended up eating (among other things).
Wasurechattari suru - 忘れちゃったりする - I end up forgetting (among other things).

～ちゃったり is **not** a standalone word. It attaches directly to verbs and appears here only because learners often mistake it for a stem.

～gatera ～がてら:

A conjunctive suffix (not a standalone word) that attaches to nouns or verb ます -stems to mean "while doing X / on the occasion of X / as a chance to also do X." It expresses dual purpose: doing one action and using it as an opportunity to do another.

1) Noun + がてら → "while… / on my way… / as part of…"

Sanpo gatera, konbini ni yotta.
散歩がてら、コンビニに寄った。
I stopped by the convenience store while taking a **walk**.

> Note: yoru can mean either "night" (夜) or "to stop by" (寄る) depending on the kanji. The te and ta forms (寄って and 寄った) always come from the verb 寄る, never from 夜 (yoru).

Kaimono gatera, tegami o dashite kita.
買い物がてら、手紙を出してきた。
I mailed a letter while I was out **shopping**.

> Note: 出す (dasu) literally means "to put out" as discussed in Part IV, but when used with letters or mail, it naturally means "to mail."
> 出した (dashita) = "mailed it."
> When combined as 出してきた (dashite kita), it adds the nuance of going somewhere to mail it and then returning, a common way to describe short round-trip errands in Japanese.

Here, the noun expresses the main activity, and がてら adds the nuance of "since I'm already doing that, I'll also do this."

2) Verb ます-stem + がてら → "while doing X / on the occasion of X"

Hakubutsukan o mi-gatera, kōen o sanpo shita.
博物館を見がてら、公園を散歩した。
I took a walk in the park while visiting the **museum**.

> Note: Hakubutsukan is quite a mouthful for museum. Here is a breakdown of the word that best explains how it came to be. 博 (haku) stands for broad, extensive, or learned. It appears in 博士 "doctor / PhD," meaning "extensive knowledge." 物 (butsu / mono) implies a thing or object. 館 (kan) is a building, hall, or institution. It is used in 図書館 "library," 美術館 "art museum," 体育館 "gymnasium."
>
> So 博物館 literally means: a hall of extensive things → a museum. It's a compound noun, not a stem, not a suffix, not a pattern, just a vocabulary word.

Iki-gatera, **hana** o katte iku yo.
行きがてら、**花**を買っていくよ。
I'll buy **flowers** on my way there.

行きがてら almost always implies physical movement toward a destination. In addition, verb-stem + がてら is less common than noun + がてら, but fully natural.

～gatte ～がって:

The stem attaches to certain adjectives and verbs to describe someone else's feelings or desires, specifically feelings that the speaker can observe externally (body language, behavior, tone, etc.). It does not describe your own internal feelings. It is used only for third-person (or sometimes second-person) when the emotion is visible.

It often carries meanings like:
- "acting like they want…" "seems to feel…"
- "is showing signs of…" "is behaving as if…"

This stem appears in forms like:
- ～gatte iru ～がっている (currently showing the feeling)
- ～gatta ～がった (showed the feeling – past tense)
- ～gari ～がり (tendency to feel) — related but separate
- ～garu ～がる (base verb form)

These are classic "emotion/physical state" adjectives that naturally form ～がって:
- samui 寒い → samugatte iru 寒がっている (seems cold)
- kowai 怖い → kowagatte iru 怖がっている (seems scared)
- hazukashī 恥ずかしい → hazukashigatte iru 恥ずかしがっている (feeling embarrassed)
- hoshī 欲しい → hoshigatte iru 欲しがっている (third person wanting it)
- itai 痛い → itagatte iru 痛がっている (in pain)

1) Observable desire

Otōto wa **atarashii** gēmu o hoshigatte iru.
弟は**新しい**ゲームを欲しがっている。
My little brother seems to want a **new** game.
(English translation: My little brother wants a new game.)

2) Observable fear

Kodomotachi wa inu o **kowagatte** iru.
子どもたちは犬を**怖がって**いる。
The children are **scared** of the dog.

Note: ～tachi (～たち) is a pluralizing suffix mainly used for people (and sometimes animals). It does not simply mean "plural" the way English s does — instead, it creates a group centered around that noun.
So: 子ども → 子どもたち (kodomo → kodomo-tachi)
→ the children / the kids / the group of children
It highlights that we're talking about a set of individuals, not just the abstract concept of "children."

Important: ～たち is not used for objects (× hon-tachi for "books"), and it does not change the meaning of the base noun beyond indicating a group.

3) Acting embarrassed

Kare wa sono **hanashi** o suru to hazukashigatta.
彼はその話をすると恥ずかしがった。
He got embarrassed when we **talked** about that.

4) Showing pain

Kanojo wa **ashi** o itagatte iru.
彼女は足を痛がっている。
She's acting like her **leg** hurts.
(English translation: Her leg is hurting.)

5) Acting cold

Neko ga samugatte iru.
猫が寒がっている。
The **cat** seems cold.

～nakute ～なくて:

This stem is the negative te-form of ～ない. It makes a verb or adjective negative, and then connects that negative state to what comes next. It does not mean a neutral "and." Instead, it expresses:

- "not…and (as a result)"
- "because not…"
- "in that (negative) state…"

For example:
1) Reason / "because not…"

Okane ga nakute, ikenai.
お金がなくて、行けない。
I don't have **money**, so I can't go.
("Because I don't have money…")

> Note: The forms ～eru (～える) / ～enai (～えない) and ～rareru (～られる) / ～rarenai (～られない) are the potential forms of verbs. They express "can" and "can't." These patterns were previously discussed in Part VI: Voice & Agency, where the potential form is explained in detail. Here, just remember that 行けない (ikenai) means "can't go," not "won't go", which is 行かない (ikanai).

2) Result / "not…and (so)…"

Jikan ga nakute, **isoida**.
時間がなくて、**急いだ**。
I didn't have time, so I **rushed**.

3) Negative state.

Hazukashiku nakute, yokatta.
恥ずかしくなくて、よかった。
I wasn't **embarrassed**, and that was good.

> Note: Why are there two "ku" sounds in hazukashiku nakute? There are two separate reasons, and each word contributes its own く.
>
> a) The first く comes from the adjective 恥ずかしい. The rule states that i-adjectives cannot attach directly to ない. To make an i-adjective negative, you must first change ～い → ～く.
> - hazukashii 恥ずかしい → hazukashiku 恥ずかしく
> - 恥ずかしく + ない → hazukashikunai 恥ずかしくない
>
> So the first く belongs to 恥ずかしい.
>
> b) The second く comes from the adjective nai (ない). The word ない is also an i-adjective. All i-adjectives form their te-form as ～くて.
> - nai ない → nakute なくて
>
> Put together:
> - hazukashii 恥ずかしい → hazukashiku 恥ずかしく
> - nai ない → nakute なくて
> - 恥ずかしく + なくて → hazukashiku nakute 恥ずかしくなくて

There is no extra く. You are simply seeing two different adjectives, each using their required "ku" form before attaching the next element.

4) Negative action causing something to happen.

Asagohan o tabenakute, **onaka ga suita**.
朝ごはんを食べなくて、**お腹がすいた**。
I didn't eat breakfast, so I got **hungry**.

Note: The word すいた (suita) is the past tense of the verb 空く (suku), which means "to become empty." On its own, suita simply means "became empty." When paired with お腹 (onaka, stomach), the meaning becomes idiomatic: to become hungry/became hungry.

～nara ～なら:

It's a topic-setting conditional. Rather than describing a natural result (like ～ba / ～ば) or a sequence of events (like ～tara / ～たら), ～なら responds to information; something the listener said, implied, or asked about. It expresses: "if it's true that…" / "if it's the case that…" / "if we're talking about…" / "As for that thing you mentioned…" Here are the core functions of ～なら:

1) Responding to information the listener gives. This is the heart of なら.

a) Nihongo ga **muzukashī** desu.
日本語が**難しい**です。
Japanese is **difficult**.

b) Muzukashī nara, **tetsudaimasu** yo.
難しいなら、**手伝います**よ。
If it's difficult (as you say), **I'll help you**.

The speaker is reacting to what the other person said.

2) "If it's about X…" (topic-based conditional). なら can introduce a topic and give advice or suggestions.

Tōkyō nara, **bijutsukan** ga ōi desu yo.
東京なら、**美術館**が多いですよ。
If it's Tokyo you're talking about, there are lots of **(art) museums**.

This doesn't mean "if Tokyo happens." It means "as for Tokyo…"

3) Giving advice based on the listener's situation. なら is perfect for conditional suggestions.

Jikan ga nai nara, takushī ni shita hō ga ī yo.
時間がないなら、タクシーにしたほうがいいよ。
If you don't have time, you should take a taxi.

The advice is tied to the listener's condition.

> Note: In タクシー (takushii), the u sound in ku is not fully pronounced in natural speech. It becomes very weak, almost silent, because Japanese often devoices the vowel u between voiceless consonants like k and sh. So even though it's written ta-ku-shii, it usually sounds closer to: takshii (a light, quick "ku"). The vowel is still there, just softened. This is the same natural reduction you hear in words like: すき (suki) and つき (tsuki).
>
> While we're on the same topic, in natural Japanese speech, the i in shi often becomes very light or nearly silent when followed by ta. In the example above, shita (した) often sounds closer to shta (a quick, blended sound).

4) Soft, polite, or formal emphasis. ならば is the more formal version.

Hitsuyō nara ba, renraku shite kudasai.
必要ならば、連絡してください。
If it's **necessary**, please contact me.

(This format was already used in the ～ば section.)

Simply, ～なら is used to respond to information, give advice based on the listener's situation, or introduce a topic. It attaches to:

- nouns

日本人なら / Nihonjin nara (if you're Japanese)

- na-adjectives

便利なら / benri nara (if it's convenient)

- verbs (plain form)

行くなら / iku nara (if you're going / if you plan to go)

- i-adjectives (plain form)

暑いなら / atsui nara (if it's hot)

It's extremely simple. There are no stem changes, no conjugation gymnastics.

~sō ~そう:

A stem that expresses either appearance ("looks/seems…") or imminence ("about to…"). It attaches to verb stems and adjective stems to show what appears likely or what seems on the verge of happening. There are two major types:

1) Imminent-action そう ("about to…") Attaches to verb stems to show that something feels close to happening.

Ame ga furi-sō da.
雨が降りそうだ。
It looks like it's about to **rain**.

> Note: You should say Ame ga furi-sō da (casual) or Ame ga furi-sō desu (polite). While ori-sō da is a valid form meaning "looks like it will break," it is wrong for rain. If you accidentally say ori-sō, a Japanese speaker will understand your intended meaning, but the correct form for "about to rain" is always furi-sō da.

Naki-sō ni natta.
泣きそうになった。
I felt like I was about to **cry**.

This is the same ~そう used in the previous entry, functioning here as a dynamic marker of imminent action rather than static appearance, which explicitly captures a vivid sense of anticipation or urgency.

> Note: The base verb for "cry" is: 泣く (naku). In the example above it is presented in its ます-stem to show imminent action:
> - 泣く (naku) → base verb
> - 泣き (naki) → ます-stem
> - 泣きそう (naki-sō) → "feel like crying" / "about to cry"
> - 泣きそうになった → "I felt like crying"

> Note: Why natta なった (past tense) appears in 泣きそうになった. When describing a momentary change of state, ~になる almost always uses the past tense. Even if the emotion or urge is spontaneous, the shift into that state is treated as a completed moment, something that happened. So in: 泣きそうになった (I felt like crying), the grammar is:

- 泣きそう = "feel like crying / about to cry"
- ～になる = "to become (that state)"
- ～になった = "became (that state)" → the moment the feeling hit you

It doesn't mean "I cried." It means: "There was a moment when I felt like crying." Japanese marks that moment with the past tense.

2) Appearance そう ("looks/seems…") Attaches to adjective stems to describe how something appears.

Kono kēki wa oishi-sō.
このケーキはおいしそう。
This cake looks delicious.

Kare wa **isogashi**-sōda.
彼は**忙し**そうだ。
He seems **busy**.
This そう expresses visual or intuitive impression.

How ～そう attaches to stems:
1) Verb stems → imminent-action そう ("about to…")
Attach そう to the verb stem (the ます-stem).

- furu 降る → furi-sō 降りそう (about to rain)
- naku 泣く → naki-sō 泣きそう (about to cry)
- ochiru 落ちる → ochi-sō 落ちそう (about to fall)

Negative form (verb):
Use ～ nasasō ～なさそう(doesn't seem like…)

- furanasasō 降らなさそう (It doesn't look like it will rain.)

Exception (する / 来る):

- suru する → shi-sō しそう (Seems likely to do (something)
- kuru 来る → ki-sō 来そう（きそう） (Looks like it's coming…)

2) Adjective stems → appearance そう ("looks/seems…")
With i-adjectives, drop the final い, then add そう.

- oishī おいしい → oishi-sō おいしそう (looks delicious)
- samui さむい → samu-sō さむそう (looks cold)

With na-adjectives, attach そう directly to the adjective stem.

- shizuka しずか → shizuka-sō しずかそう (seems quiet)
- taihen たいへん → taihen-sō たいへんそう (seems tough)

Negative form (adjectives):

Use ～ku nasasō ～くなさそう.

- oishiku nasasō おいしくなさそう (It doesn't look tasty.)

Sidebar: Common Exceptions For ～sō

Most ～そう forms follow predictable patterns:

- verb stem + そう for "about to…"
- adjective stem + そう for "looks/seems…"

However, a few words don't follow the standard pattern because of historical forms, irregular stems, or sound changes that developed naturally over time. These are not mistakes or special rules—just natural evolutions of the language. Because learners encounter them frequently, they are worth memorizing as "common exceptions."

1) いい → よさそう (looks good)
This is the most famous exception.

2) ない → なさそう (doesn't seem to exist / doesn't seem likely)
Used for both verbs and adjectives.

3) ～そうに / ～そうな
Used to modify verbs or nouns.

- ureshi-sō ni warau うれしそうに笑う (laugh happily / looking happy)
- sabishi-sōna hito さびしそうな人 (a person who looks lonely)

Sidebar: Common Learner Mistakes

Even though ～そう follows clear patterns, learners often mix up the two major types ("about to…" vs. "looks/seems…"), or they apply the stem rules too literally. Because ～そう attaches differently to verbs and adjectives—and because a few forms behave irregularly—certain mistakes appear again and again. The following list highlights the most common pitfalls so you can avoid them from the start.

Mistake 1: Using ～そう with the dictionary form of verbs:
Incorrect: naku sō 泣くそう (looks like they're going to cry)
Correct: naki-sō 泣きそう (use the stem)

Mistake 2: Forgetting the いい → よさそう exception. いいそう is never correct.

Mistake 3: Using ～そう for hearsay. Learners sometimes think そう = "I heard that…".
That's ～そうだ (hearsay), a different grammar point.

End Sidebar

~sugiru ~すぎる:

A bound helper verb meaning "too much / excessively," and must attach to a verb stem or adjective stem. It is not a standalone word. Even though learners often think of sugiru as a "word," grammatically it is a helper verb that:

- attaches directly to stems
- cannot appear by itself
- cannot take particles before it
- cannot be used independently as "sugiru" in a sentence

Japanese dictionaries classify すぎる as a 補助動詞 (auxiliary verb). They **must** attach to another word to function. It is bound, just like: ~nagara, ~gatera, ~tsuide ni, ~yasui / ~nikui, ~tai, ~tagaru.

The meaning of ~すぎる depends on attachment. It attaches to:

- verb stems

tabesugiru 食べすぎる → eat too much
nomisugiru 飲みすぎる → drink too much

- adjective stems

takasugiru 高すぎる → too expensive
shizukasugiru 静かすぎる → too quiet

1) Verb + ~sugiru (too much / excessively)

Tabesugita.
食べすぎた。
I ate too much.

This is the most classic and intuitive example. Verb stem tabe- + sugiru → "to over-eat."

2) Adjective stem + ~sugiru (too ~)

Kono **kutsu** wa takasugiru.
この靴は高すぎる。
These **shoes** are too expensive.

Adjective stem taka- + sugiru → "too expensive." For i-adjectives, drop the final い : 高い → 高すぎる. For na-adjectives, attach directly to the stem: 静か → 静かすぎる (shizukasugiru) / too quiet.

~tara ～たら:

A conditional form built from the past tense that implies if / then. English splits these meanings into 'if,' 'when,' and 'after,' but Japanese uses ～たら for all of them depending on context. But ～たら doesn't just mean "if/when." It means "after X happens, then Y." It expresses a condition that becomes true once the first action or event is complete. It's both conditional and temporal at the same time.

Here are four major uses:

1) HYPOTHETICAL "IF":

- If it rains → I'll go home.
  Moshi ame ga futtara, watashi wa ie ni kaerimasu.
  もし雨が降ったら、私は家に帰ります。

2) NATURAL "WHEN":

- When I get home → I'll call you.
  Ie ni kaettara denwa shimasu.
  家に帰ったら電話します。

3) UNEXPECTED DISCOVERY:

- After I opened the door → there was a cat.
  Doa o aketara, neko ga ita.
  ドアを開けたら、猫がいた。

4) POLITE INVITATIONS / SUGGESTIONS:

- If you like → please go ahead.
  Yokattara, dōzo.
  よかったら、どうぞ。

All of these are ～たら. In addition, even though ～たら uses the past tense (～た), it does not mean the action is in the past. The past tense simply marks the completion of the condition.

Example:
Ame ga futtara, kaerimasu.
雨が降ったら、帰ります。
If/when it rains (after it starts raining), I'll go home.
The rain isn't in the past — it's the trigger.

Each conditional has a personality:

- ～ば = logical, abstract
- ～と = automatic, natural consequence
- ～なら = assumption-based, "if it's true that…"
- ～たら = real-life, event-based, practical

～たら is the most human conditional. It's used for everyday situations, decisions, and reactions to real events.

～tara ii ～たらいい:

Suggestion / "Should / Why don't you…?" / "It would be good if…" It is another common way to give friendly, practical advice, suggestions, or gentle recommendations.

～たらいい overlaps with ～ばいい, but it feels more conversational, softer, and more "real-life" because ～たら is an event-based conditional ("after X happens…"). The literal meaning is: "If you do X (after you do X), it will be good." But in natural Japanese, it simply means:

- "You should…"
- "Why don't you try…?"
- "It might be good to…"

This pattern is extremely common in everyday speech. Sample sentences are:

1) Friendly advice:
Motto yasundara ii yo.
もっと休んだらいいよ。
You should rest more.

2) Suggesting a solution:
Wakaranakattara, **sensei** ni kiitara ii.
わからなかったら、**先生**に聞いたらいい。
If you don't understand, you should ask the **teacher**.

Note: The ら in わからなかったら (wakaranakattara) is not random. It's the conditional marker of the ～たら form.
Here's the structure:
a) わかる (wakaru) — to understand
b) わからない (wakaranai) — to not understand

c) わからなかった (wakaranakatta) — did not understand (past negative)

d) わからなかったら (wakaranakattara)
→ "if you didn't understand / if you don't understand (in that moment)"

In English, we translate this as "if you don't understand," even though Japanese uses the past form. The ら is simply the conditional ending attached to the past form of the verb.

This is why:

- iku 行く → 行った → ittara 行ったら (If I go)
- taberu 食べる → 食べた → tabetara 食べたら (when you eat)
- wakaranai わからない → わからなかった → wakaranakattara わからなかったら (if you don't understand)

Even though it uses the past form (わからなかった), the meaning is not past. It simply follows the rule: past form + ら = conditional ("if / when").

3) Soft recommendation:
Jikan ga attara, **sanpo** <u>shitara ii</u> yo.
時間があったら、**散歩**<u>したらいい</u>よ。
If you have time, <u>you should (do it)</u> take a **walk**.

4) Emotional reassurance:
Shinpai dattara, denwa <u>shitara ii</u> yo.
心配だったら、電話<u>したらいい</u>よ。
If you're **worried**, <u>you should (do it)</u> call.

Demo でも:

As a conjunction, demo means "but / however." But in Part V: Excess & Combination, we focus on a different usage: でも as "even / despite / including." This でも attaches to nouns, pronouns, and question words to express unexpected inclusion, generous allowance, or "even X…" nuance.

1) でも meaning "even / despite / including." Noun + demo → "even X / despite X."

For example:
Kodomo demo <u>dekiru</u>.
子どもでも<u>できる</u>。
Even a **child** <u>can do it</u>.

Ame demo iku.
雨でも行く。
I'll go even if it's **raining**.

This でも highlights that the situation is not enough to stop the action or that the subject is included unexpectedly.

2) Question-word + demo → "any / every / no matter what." This is one of the most powerful "combination" uses.

- dare だれ (who) → だれでも = anyone / everyone
- itsu いつ (when) → いつでも = anytime
- doko どこ (where) → どこでも = anywhere
- nan なん (what) → なんでも = anything
- ikura いくら (how much) → いくらでも = as much as you want
- dore どれ (which one) → どれでも = whichever / any of them

Sample sentences:
Itsu demo **kite** kudasai.
いつでも**来て**ください。
Come anytime.

Nandemo **kiite**.
なんでも**聞いて**。
Ask me anything.

Note: なんでも can also mean "whatever / anything is fine," depending on context. For example: Nandemo ii yo / なんでもいいよ / Anything is fine. / Whatever is okay.

Note: 聞く (kiku) is used for both "to listen/hear" and "to ask." The kanji is the same, and the て-form 聞いて (kiite) is also identical. Japanese distinguishes the meanings through context:

- ongaku o kiite 音楽を聞いて → listening to music
- sensei ni kiite 先生に聞いて → asking the teacher

Because the form is identical, learners should rely on the particle and situation to interpret the meaning.

Historically, both meanings come from the idea of directing attention toward sound or information:

- Listening → directing attention to sound
- Asking → directing attention to information you want to receive

So Japanese kept both meanings under one verb.

Doko demo ii yo.
どこでもいいよ。
Anywhere is fine.
Here, でも creates a sense of open possibility or unrestricted choice.

Dore demo ii yo. Nandemo **erande**.
どれでもいいよ。なんでも**選んで**。
Any of them is fine. **Pick** whatever you like.

Gurai ぐらい / Kurai くらい:

These forms have two unrelated meanings: (1) approximation ("about"), which belongs in Part VII, and (2) degree/extent ("to the point that"), which belongs in Part V.

In this section, we are focusing on the degree/extent meaning of くらい / ぐらい, the one that expresses intensity ("to the point that…"). This use has nothing to do with approximation. Instead, it describes how strong, extreme, or overwhelming something feels. It attaches to verbs, adjectives, or entire clauses to show the extent of an emotion, action, or state. For example:

Shinu kurai tsukareta.
死ぬくらい疲れた。
I'm tired to the point of **dying**.

Nakitai gurai ureshī.
泣きたいぐらい嬉しい。
I'm so happy I **could cry** (want to cry).

> Note: くらい and ぐらい are interchangeable. ぐらい is slightly more colloquial, but both are used in all contexts.

These meanings express intensity, degree, or excess.

Kurai くらい: See entry for "Gurai ぐらい / Kurai くらい" above.

Made まで:

Meaning: limit / endpoint; in some contexts, expresses unexpected inclusion ("even"). A particle that attaches to nouns, verbs, or time expressions—not a conjunction.

1. Limit / endpoint ("until")

   3-ji made matsu - 3時まで待つ - Wait **until** 3 o'clock.
2. Extent / inclusion ("even")

   Kodomo made naita - 子供まで泣いた - **Even** the children cried.
3. Range ("up to / as far as")

   Tōkyō made iku - 東京まで行く - Go **as far as** Tokyo.

> Note on learner confusion: Sometimes learners think まで is acting like a conjunction when they see forms such as:
>
> - ～までに ("by the time…")
> - ～まで ("until… happens")
>
> Example:
> 雨が降るまで待つ。
> "Wait until it rains."
>
> This feels like a conjunction because it introduces a condition, but grammatically it is still a particle attaching to a verb phrase, not a clause-connector.

Mo も:

The Particle of "Even," "Also," and Emotional Extension. Learners constantly misunderstand も, especially in negative sentences. And this framework is perfect for showing how も shifts emotional tone.

も expands or intensifies the scope of what's being talked about; sometimes adding, sometimes emphasizing, sometimes minimizing.

- Miru ki mo nai - 見る気もない → "I don't even feel like watching."

Note: Ki 気 was covered in depth in section IV as a nuance for feeling, mood, inclination, motivation.

The structure for ki 気 is:

見る気 = the feeling of wanting to watch

見る気も = even the feeling of wanting to watch

しない = do not have / do not do

Put together:

見る気もしない。

→ "I don't even have the feeling to watch it."

→ "I don't even feel like watching it."

The mo も is the key.

It adds the nuance of zero interest, not even a tiny bit, absolutely no desire.

- Okane mo nai - お金もない → "I don't even have money."
- Jikan mo aru - 時間もある → "I also have time."
- Kimi mo kuru - 君も来る？ → "Are you coming too?"

Ra (ら):

One of the most elegant patterns in Japanese grammar for expressing a hypothetical condition. Let's unpack it in a way that makes the whole system click by using the verb furu (to fall – as in rain, snow). Here, we start with the progressive / continuous verb form:

Ame ga futte iru.

雨 が 降って いる 。

It is raining.

This is the conditional form of the same verb:

Ame ga futt<u>ara</u>

雨 が 降ったら

→ "If it rains…"

→ "When it rains…"

→ "What if it rains…"

Japanese uses the past tense + ら to express a hypothetical condition.

- Ittara 行ったら = if/when I go
- Tabetara 食べたら = if/when you eat
- Yondara 読んだら = if/when you read
- Futtara ふったら = if/when it rains

Futtara ふったら does not mean "if it rained (in the past)." It means "if it rains (in the future)."

Moshi **ame ga futtara**, dekakenai.
もし**雨がふったら**、出かけない。
If it **rains**, I won't go out.

Note that the ra (ら) in futtara implies "if," so why add the word moshi (もし)? This is exactly where Japanese shows its subtle, almost musical layering of nuance. Because もし doesn't change the grammar — it changes the tone. Although not necessary, もし adds a feeling of:

- "What if…"
- "Suppose…"
- "In case…"
- "Let's imagine that…"

It does not create the conditional — it emphasizes it.

Here is a side-by-side comparison:
Ame ga futtara, ikanai.
雨がふったら、行かない。
If it rains, I won't go.
→ Neutral, factual, straightforward.

Moshi ame ga futtara, ikanai.
もし雨がふったら、行かない。
What if it rains? Then I won't go.
→ More speculative, imagining the possibility.

Sae さえ:

A strong "even" particle that marks the outer edge of expectation. It highlights something surprising, extreme, or beyond what one would normally assume. Used to emphasize that if even this minimal or unexpected case is true, then everything else follows.

さえ is the strongest "even" among the three: demo (でも), made (まで), sae (さえ). Here's the hierarchy in natural Japanese:

- でも → mild "even". Used for simple inclusion or light contrast.
  Kodomo demo dekiru - 子供でもできる - Even a child can do it.

- まで → "even" with a sense of extent. It stretches the boundary of what you'd expect.
  Kodomo made naita - 子供まで泣いた - Even the children cried.

- さえ → strong, pointed "even". It highlights the outer edge of possibility.
  Mizu sae nomenai - 水さえ飲めない - I can't even drink water.
  (Meaning: If I can't even do this minimal thing…)

Shika nai しかない:

Emphatic limitation: "only," in the sense of "nothing but." A particle that highlights restriction, scarcity, or insufficiency. Used with a negative verb, しか expresses that this is the only option, amount, or possibility, and it's less than expected or desired.

しか～ない works both with and without a word in between, and this flexibility is actually one of its defining features. しか attaches directly to the thing being limited: a noun, a number/amount, a verb in dictionary form, a verb in て-form, a clause. You will naturally see しか appear right before whatever is being restricted, and the negative verb may be right next to it or farther away (often ～ない, but sometimes ～ません, ～なかった, etc.).

1) Amount / quantity limitation:
Okane ga **sen'en** shika nai.
お金が**千円**しかない。
I only have 1,000 yen.
(literally: "There is nothing but **1,000 yen**.")

2) Time limitation:
Kyō wa **ichi-jikan** shika benkyō shinakatta.
今日は**一時間**しか勉強しなかった。
I studied for only **one hour** today.
(= less than I should have)

> Note: Why this sentence does not mean "didn't study." Sentence: Kyō wa ichi-jikan shika benkyō shinakatta / Today, I studied for only one hour. At first glance, learners see shinakatta and think: "shinakatta = didn't do → didn't study." But that's not what's happening here. The key is shika.
>
> しか (shika) always pairs with a negative verb, but the meaning becomes positive: Examples:
>
> - 100 en shika nai. → I only have 100 yen.
> - Hitotsu shika tabenakatta. → I only ate one.

- Nihongo shika hanasenai. → I can only speak Japanese.

The negative verb is grammatical, not literal. The negative is required by shika, but the meaning is controlled by shika, not by the verb ending.

3) Option limitation:

Koko kara iku **hōhō** wa densha shika nai.
ここから行く**方法**は電車しかない。
The only **way** to get there from here is by train.
(= no other options exist)

Note: Densha 電車 means electric train. Literally:

- 電 = electric
- 車 = vehicle

It does not mean "train" in the broad, general sense. It specifically refers to electric trains, which includes: commuter trains, subway trains, light rail, trams (in some regions). But it does not include: diesel trains, steam trains, and Shinkansen (bullet train). It can mean "the train system" in casual speech. In everyday conversation, 電車 often just means "the train you normally ride," even if the speaker isn't thinking about the technical distinction.

4) People limitation:

Tetsudatte kureru **hito** wa kare shika inai.
手伝ってくれる**人**は彼しかいない。
He's the only **person** who can help.
(= no one else is available)

Note: In Japanese, kureru くれる is a verb meaning:

- "to give (to me / to someone in my in-group)"
- "to do something for me" (when attached to another verb)

When you attach くれる to a て-form verb, it expresses: someone does that action for me (or for the speaker's benefit.) So:

- tetsudau 手伝う = to help
- tetsudatte kureru 手伝ってくれる = "help (me) for my benefit" → "help me"

This is why tetsudatte kureru hito (手伝ってくれる人) means: "a person who helps me." Literally: "a person who gives me helping." Without くれる, 手伝う人 could mean "a person who helps (someone)," but not necessarily "me."

5) Action limitation:
Yasumu jikan ga hotondo nakute, neru shika nakatta.
休む時間がほとんどなくて、寝るしかなかった。
I barely had any time to **rest**, so sleeping was my only option.
(= nothing else I could do)

Note: Hotondo ほとんど is an adverb that means: almost all, nearly all, most. In the example provided, it is paired with the negative nakute (なくて) which makes the phrase almost none or hardly any. Other nuances include: nearly / almost (degree, not quantity) and virtually / practically (formal writing.)

But it also has a second role: adverbial noun (fukushi-teki meishi / 副詞的名詞). ほとんど can also behave like a noun when followed by の:

- hotondo no hito ほとんどの人 = most people
- hotondo no jikan ほとんどの時間 = most of the time
- hotondo no mondai ほとんどの問題 = most of the problems

In these cases, it's functioning as a noun that modifies another noun, similar to:

- takusan no たくさんの (lots of)
- sukoshi no 少しの (a little)
- ōku no 多くの (many)

So grammatically, dictionaries classify it as: 副詞 (adverb), 副詞的名詞 (adverbial noun). But the adverb usage is the primary one. Common misuse: ほとんど is not used to mean "mostly" in the sense of "mainly because…" (that's omoni / 主に / おもに).

6) Emphatic insufficiency:
Kon'na **sukoshi** shika tabete inai no ni, mō onaka-ippai?
こんな**少し**しか食べていないのに、もうお腹いっぱい？
You only ate this **little**, and you're already full?

Note: Kon'na こんな means "this kind of / like this," not simply "this." It modifies a noun to show degree or type. In こんな少し, it means "this little" or "such a small amount."

しか always requires a negative verb. Dake だけ can stand alone, but しか cannot. This is why Japanese says "Pan shika tabenai" パンしか食べない, not "Pan shika taberu" パンしか食べる.

To と:

This core conjunctive particle is used to connect nouns, people, and actions in a way that expresses combination, pairing, listing, or joint participation. It is one of the most fundamental "linking" particles in Japanese.

1. Noun + と + Noun → "A and B".
This is the most basic use: linking two nouns as a pair or set.
- pan to batā パンとバター → bread and butter
- inu to neko 犬と猫 → dogs and cats
- ani to ane 兄と姉 → older brother and older sister

Pan to **tamago** o kaimashita.
パンと**卵**を買いました。
I bought bread and **eggs**.
Nuance: と lists items as a complete, closed set; unlike や, which gives an incomplete list.

2. Person + と + Verb → "with (someone)".
When と follows a person, it expresses doing something together or in the company of someone.
- tomodachi to hanasu 友だちと話す → to talk with a friend
- kazoku to **ryokō** shita 家族と**旅行**した → I **traveled** with my family
- sensei to **sōdan** suru 先生と**相談**する → to **consult** with the teacher

Tomodachi to **eiga** o mita.
友だちと**映画**を見た。
I watched a **movie** with a friend.
Nuance: と marks the other participant in the action, a joint or reciprocal involvement.

Kare to kanojo wa issho ni **hataraite** iru.
彼と彼女はいっしょに**働い**ている。
He and she are **working** together.
Nuance: と links the pair as a unit.

3. と for paired actions or simultaneous states.
Used to link two actions or states that occur together or form a natural pair.
- Haru ni naru to, **sakura** ga saku. 春になると、**桜**が咲く。→ When spring comes, the **cherry blossoms** bloom.

- Kare wa kuru to <u>sugu</u> ni kaetta. 彼は来ると<u>すぐ</u>に帰った。→ He came and <u>immediately</u> left.

Sidebar: Why と sometimes feels like a conditional (“when X, Y happens”)

Even though と is best known as the “and / with” particle, it also appears in sentences where the English translation uses “when” or “whenever.” This is not a separate grammar pattern. It is the same と, used in a different structural environment.

When と connects two clauses, Japanese interprets the relationship as:

- a natural sequence
- an automatic result
- something that always happens when the first action occurs

This creates a meaning like:

- “when X happens, Y naturally follows”
- “whenever X, Y”
- “as soon as X, Y”

Examples:

Botan o **osu** to, doa ga [hiraku].
ボタンを押すと、ドアが[開く]。
If you **press** the button, the door [opens].
(Pressing → opening: automatic result)

Ie ni kaeru to, ame ga furi [hajimeta].
家に帰ると、雨が降り[始めた]。
When I got **home**, [it started] raining.
(Arrival → onset of rain: sequential timing)

This と does not express a hypothetical condition. It expresses a linked action or natural consequence, which is why it belongs in Part V, not in the conditional section. It is different from:

- ～tara ～たら (general “if / when”)
- ～ba ～ば (logical “if”)
- ～nara ～なら (contextual “if it’s the case that…”)

と is not about possibility, it’s about what happens next.

End Sidebar

PART VI: VOICE & AGENCY (STRUCTURAL STEMS)

Key stems and nuances in this section:

- ～eru ～える → Potential-family only (can do, able to do, cannot do)
- ～ra ～ら → Plural marker / group identity
- ～rare ～られ → Passive-family only (to be ---ed)
- ～sase ～させ → Causative (to make/let someone do something)
- ～tachi ～たち → group identity, collective agency, or belonging
- kanjiru 感じる → Experiential voice (excluding to think and to know)

Vocabulary to review:

demasu	出ます	go out, appear, attend
giron	議論	discussion, debate
jōshi	上司	boss
kaku	書く	write
kakeru	書ける	can write
kanjiru	感じる	to feel, to sense, to perceive
katazukeru	片づける	to tidy up, to clean up, to put things in order
kurai (i-adjective)	暗い	dark, dim, gloomy
matsuri	祭り	festival
niku	肉	meat
ochiru	落ちる	to fall, drop, come off, decline, fail (an exam)
odoru	踊る	to dance
oshidasu	押し出す	to push out, to thrust forward, to assert, to project outward
osoreru	恐れる	to fear, to dread
otōto	弟	younger brother
oyogu	泳ぐ	swim
shikaru	叱る	to scold
shimeru	閉める	close
shizen	自然	nature / natural
tatsu	立つ	to stand / to get up (onto one's feet)
tobu	飛ぶ	to jump / to fly
tsuyoku	強く	strongly
utau	歌う	to sing

warau	笑う	to laugh
zangyō	残業	overtime work

Diving further into the stems and nuances

~eru ~える:

The ～える form is the potential form of Japanese verbs. The structural transformation that expresses ability ("can do") or inability ("cannot do"). It is one of the core voice-and-agency patterns because it changes the subject's capacity to perform an action, not the action itself.

The potential form expresses:

- ability: "can ___"
- possibility: "is able to ___"
- inability: "cannot ___" (～えない / ～られない)

It answers the question:
"Is the subject capable of doing the action?"

Japanese has two patterns, depending on the verb type.
1) Godan verbs → ～える / ～えない
The final sound shifts to the e-row, then takes る.

- 書く → 書ける / 書けない (kaku → kakeru / kakenai)
- 行く → 行ける / 行けない (iku → ikeru / ikenai)
- 読む → 読める / 読めない (yomu → yomeru / yomenai)
- 話す → 話せる / 話せない (hanasu → hanaseru / hanasenai)
- 飲む → 飲める / 飲めない (nomu → nomeru / nomenai)

2) Ichidan verbs → ～られる / ～られない
Attach られる to the stem.

- 食べる → 食べられる / 食べられない (taberu → taberareru / taberarenai)
- 見る → 見られる / 見られない (miru → mirareru / mirarenai)
- 起きる → 起きられる / 起きられない (okiru → okirareru / okirarenai)

This ～られる looks identical to the passive form, but the meaning is different.

The ~rare entry below covers the passive meaning; this entry covers the ability meaning.

> Note: What are ichidan and godan verbs? Japanese verbs come in two main groups. You don't need to memorize every detail right now, just the basic idea.

a) Ichidan verbs (also called "ru-verbs").

These verbs end in ～る, and the part before る **stays the same** when you conjugate. For example:

- oshieru 教える → oshierareru 教えられる "can teach" (potential) OR "is taught" (passive), depending entirely on context.
- shimeru 閉める → shimerareru 閉められる "can close" (potential) OR "is closed" (passive), depending entirely on context.

Pattern: stem + られ (rare). This is why ichidan verbs use the full ～rare in the passive.

> Note: How Japanese speakers tell the difference. Native speakers rely on context, not form.
> For example:
> このドアは閉められる。
> - "This door can be closed." (potential)
> - "This door is closed (by someone)." (passive)
>
> Only one interpretation makes sense in the situation.
> Or:
> 日本語が教えられる。
> - "I can teach Japanese." (potential)
> - "Japanese is taught (by someone)." (passive)
>
> Again, context decides.

b) Godan verbs (also called "u-verbs")

These verbs end in u-sounds (う, く, す, む, etc.). When you conjugate them, the final sound changes. For example:

- tobu 飛ぶ (to fly) → toberu 飛べる (can fly)
- tatsu 立つ (to stand) → tateru 立てる (can stand)
- utau 歌う (to sing) → utaeru 歌える(can sing)

Pattern: e-row shift + る (ru). This is why godan verbs use ～eru, not ～rareru.

> Note: Tatsu has multiple meanings depending on the kanji: 立つ (to stand), 絶つ (to cut off), 発つ (to depart), 裁つ (to cut cloth), 建つ (to be built). The pronunciation stays the same, but the kanji determines the meaning.

3) Irregular verbs

- suru する → dekiru できる / dekinai できない
- kuru 来る → korareru 来られる / korarenai 来られない

Sample sentences (positive and negative):

a) GODAN VERBS

Kakeru yō ni natta.

書けるようにかった。

I've become **able to write** (it).

> Note: The particle に is required because なる expresses a change of state, and Japanese marks the resulting state with に.
>
> Note: 書ける and かける are unrelated. Even though they sound similar, they come from different verbs and different kanji.
>
> 書ける (kakeru)
> - Comes from 書く (kaku)
> - Meaning: "can write"
> - Category: potential form
> - Grammar: godan → e-row shift
> - Function: expresses ability
>
> かける (kakeru)
> - Base verb with many meanings depending on kanji
> - Category: lexical verb
> - Grammar: ichidan verb
> - Function: expresses actions, not ability
>
> These two are not connected in meaning or grammar.
> The "can" meaning never comes from かける.
> It comes from the potential transformation:
> - 書く → kakeru 書ける **can** write (godan → える)
> - 掛ける → kakerareru 掛けられる **can** be hung (ichidan → られる)

Kyō wa **oyogenai**.

今日は**泳げない**。

I **can't swim** today.

b) ICHIDAN VERBS

Sushi ga **taberareru**.

寿司が**食べられる**。

I **can eat** sushi.

Kyō wa **hayaku** okirarenai.

今日は**早く**起きられない。

I can't wake up **early** today.

Kyō wa **niku** ga taberarenai.
今日は**肉**が食べられない。
I can't eat **meat** today.

c) IRREGULAR VERBS

Nihongo ga dekiru yō ni natta.
日本語ができるようになった。
I've become able to speak Japanese.

> Note: The particle に is required because なる expresses a change of state, and Japanese marks the resulting state with に.
>
> Note: dekiru できる is translated as "speak" in 日本語ができるようになった because できる expresses ability in a domain, not just the ability to perform a single action. In English, we don't say "I can Japanese." We say "I can speak Japanese." Japanese leaves the verb implicit; English supplies the natural one.

Ashita wa korarenai.
明日は来られない。
I can't come **tomorrow**.

Nuance and usage notes:
• The potential form expresses capacity, not permission.
ikeru 行ける = "can go (able to go)," not "may go (allowed)."
• Ichidan potential ～られる is often shortened in speech:
taberareru 食べられる → tabereru 食べれる
mirareru 見られる → mireru 見れる
This is common but still considered casual.
• Context always disambiguates passive vs. potential:
Sakana ga taberareru 魚が食べられる
= "I can eat fish" (potential)
= "The fish is eaten" (passive)
Only one interpretation fits the situation.

～ra ～ら:

The ～ら form is a noun-attached plural marker that indicates a group of people associated with the noun. It is similar to ～たち, but with a slightly different flavor:

- ～tachi ～たち = neutral, standard plural
- ～ら = colloquial, sometimes rougher or more casual
- Often implies a group identity, not just "more than one"
- Used mostly with people, not objects

It attaches directly to nouns:

- kare 彼 → karera 彼ら (they)
- kodomo 子ども → kodomo-ra 子どもら (the kids as a group)
- sensei 先生 → sensei-ra 先生ら (the teachers, that group of teachers)

It belongs in Part VI: Voice & Agency, because it modifies who is acting, not the action itself. It is a structural noun suffix, not a verbal pattern.

1) Kare-ra wa jibun-tachi no kangae o **tsuyoku** oshidashite kita.
彼らは自分たちの考えを**強く**押し出してきた。
They **strongly** pushed forward their own ideas as a group.
Nuance: 彼ら emphasizes "that group of them," not just "they."

> Side-note: jibun 自分 does not always mean "myself." It is a reflexive pronoun that refers back to the subject of the sentence, whatever that subject is.
>
> In this sentence, the subject is kare-ra 彼ら (they), so jibun-tachi 自分たち naturally means "their own." Japanese reflexives follow the subject, not the speaker.
>
> Side-note: Why 来た (kita) is required here. 来た (kita) in 押し出してきた (oshidashite kita) is not the simple past "came." It is the helper-verb ～てくる, which expresses an action that has been developing, increasing, or accumulating up to now.
>
> 押し出してきた means "have been pushing forward (and now it shows)" — a gradual, continuing process that leads into the present moment. Without kita, the sentence would simply describe pushing forward ideas. With kita, it means they have increasingly asserted their ideas over time, and the result is felt now.
>
> This is the same nuance seen in patterns like:
>
> - Ame ga futte kita 雨が降ってきた → It has started raining (and is now happening)
> - Hito ga atsumatte kita 人が集まってきた → People have been gathering (and now they're here)
>
> So 押し出してきた = "have been asserting / pushing forward (up to now)."

2) Sensei-ra wa **kaigi** de gakusei-no shidōhō ni tsuite giron shite ita.
先生らは**会議**で学生の指導法について議論していた。
The teachers were discussing methods of guiding the students during the **meeting**.
Nuance: 先生ら frames them as "the teacher group," not just multiple teachers.

Side-note: Understanding ～ni tsuite ～について:
～について means "about," "regarding," or "concerning."
It attaches to a noun and turns that noun into the topic of discussion, analysis, or thought.

In this sentence, 学生の指導法について means "about the students' instructional methods." It is more formal and precise than simply using を, and it signals that the following action (giron suru 議論する, hanasu 話す, kangaeru 考える, etc.) is centered on that topic. ～について will be covered in depth in Part VIII: Other Important Words.

～rare ～られ:

The ～られ form is the base stem of ～rareru (～られる). It attaches to a verb stem to create a passive voice (someone is acted upon) / spontaneous, uncontrollable feelings (something "just happens" emotionally) / and a honorific, respectful form (the subject is someone respected).

1) Passive Voice. The subject receives or experiences an action:
Tomodachi ni warawareta.
友だちに笑われた。
I was laughed at by my **friend**.
Here, warawa-re-ta = "was laughed at."

Note: Why does ～rare become ～re in some verbs?
In the passive form, ichidan verbs use the full stem ～られ:

- taberu 食べる → taberareru 食べられる (to be eaten)
- miru 見る → mirareru 見られる (to be seen)
- okiru 起きる → okirareru 起きられる (passive "to be woken up" exists but is rare; the common meaning is the potential "can wake up").

So learners will see ～rare exactly as expected.
But godan verbs do not use ～rare. They use ～re instead.

- warau 笑う → warawareru 笑われる (to be laughed at)

- yomu 読む → yomareru 読まれる (to be read)
- kaku 書く → kakareru 書かれる (to be written)
- iku 行く → ikareru 行かれる (to be gone / to be affected by someone going.)

Note: Ichidan and Godan verbs are explained in the ～eru ～える section above.

2) Spontaneous / Uncontrollable Feeling. Used when an emotion or reaction arises naturally, without intention:

Sono **hanashi** o kiku to, nakare-sō ni natta.
その話を聞くと、泣かれそうになった。
When I heard that **story**, I felt like I was going to cry.

Here, nakare- expresses an involuntary emotional response.

Note: What is the ～そう in nakare-sō (泣かれそう)? The stem ～そう here expresses imminence, the sense of "about to" or "on the verge of." So in: nakare-sō ni natta / 泣かれそうになった (I felt like I was about to cry) … the ～そう attaches to the passive stem 泣かれ, creating: 泣かれそう = "seems like (I will) cry," "feels like crying is about to happen"

This is the imminent-action そう, not the "looks/seems" そう used with adjectives. A full explanation of ～そう (its types, meanings, and how it attaches to stems) appears in a dedicated entry below.

3) Honorific / Respectful Form. Used when the subject is someone respected (teacher, boss, customer, etc.):
Sensei ga koraremashita.
先生が来られました。
The teacher has arrived.
(respectful form of 来る). Here, kora-re- elevates the subject.

Note: The base verb for koraremashita is 来る (kuru); to come. Here, it is the polite past honorific.

4) Neutral Passive (non-emotional, non-honorific). Used for simple, factual passives:
Kono hon wa ōku no hito ni yomarete iru.
この本は多くの人に読まれている。
This book is being read by many people.

~sase ~させ:

The ～させform is the causative verb stem that means to make or let someone do something. It expresses causing, allowing, or compelling an action.

This stem appears before various endings to create the full causative verb family. It carries the idea of pushing the action onto someone else, either gently ("let") or forcefully ("make"), depending on context. It cannot stand alone as "sase" in a sentence. It must attach to something. It carries meaning, but it's not "activated" until you attach an ending.

These are the actual usable forms:

- saseru させる — make/let someone do
- sasenai させない — don't allow
- saseta させた — made/let someone do
- saserareru させられる — be forced to do
- saseyou させよう — let's make / try to make
- sasetan desu させたんです — explanatory "I made them do it, you see…"

All of these are させ + ending.

1. Basic pattern (past tense) attaching to a verb stem. Meaning: "caused/allowed someone to do"

Sensei wa watashi ni yomaseta.
先生は私に読ませた。
The teacher made me read.
Here, 読ませた = 読む (read) + させ (causative stem) + た (past).

2. Dictionary Form: させる. Meaning: "to make/let someone do." Form: させ + る.

Haha wa otōto ni **heya** o katazukeseru.
母は弟に**部屋**を片づけさせる。
Mom makes my little brother clean his **room**.
Nuance: neutral causative, could be strict or simply instructive.

> Note: Why you don't see "sase" in the sentence even though it's causative? Learners expect to see the causative stem ～sase, but in real sentences the causative appears as a full verb form, not the stem by itself.
> Here's what's happening:

- 片付ける (katazukeru, "to tidy up") **is an ichidan verb**
- Ichidan verbs form the causative by replacing ～ru with ～seru
- So the causative form becomes:

katazuke + seru → katazukeseru

This ～seru ending is the causative — it's simply the ichidan version of the sase pattern.

3. Negative: させない — "don't let / won't allow someone to do." Form: させ + ない

Sensei wa seito ni **keitai** o <u>tsukawasenai</u>.
先生は生徒に**携帯**を<u>使わせない</u>。
The teacher <u>doesn't allow</u> students <u>to use</u> their **(cell) phones**.

Nuance: prohibition or restriction.

Note: Why you don't see "sase" on the surface? Just like the earlier example (katazukeseru), the causative stem never appears by itself. It always merges into the full causative verb form. But here's the key difference: 使う (tsukau) **is a godan verb**. Godan verbs form the causative with:

- ～saseru in full form
- ～seru in contracted form (very common in speech and writing)

So:

1. tsukau → base verb
2. tsukawaseru → full causative ("to make/let someone use")
3. tsukawasenai → causative negative ("to not let someone use")

Notice what happened:

- The causative sase is still there, but it merges into sase + nai → sasenai
- Because 使う is a godan verb, the verb stem shifts u → a, giving tsukawa-
- This stem shift causes sase to surface as wase in the negative form
- The final surface form tsukawasenai hides the internal causative structure

4. Past: させた — "made/let someone do." Form: させ + た

Kare wa watashi ni [zenbu] **setsumei** saseta.
彼は私に[全部]**説明**させた。
He made me **explain** [everything].

Nuance: completed causative action.

5. Passive-Causative: させられる — "to be made to do (against one's will)." Form: させ + られる

Watashi wa **jōshi** ni zangyō saserareta.
私は**上司**に残業させられた。
I was made to work overtime by my **boss**."

Nuance: strong coercion; often unpleasant.

6. Volitional: させよう — "let's make (someone) do / I'll try to make them do." Form: させ + よう

Kodomo ni motto hon o yomaseyō.
子どもにもっと本を読ませよう。
Let's try to get the kids to read more.

Nuance: intention or encouragement.

7. Explanatory Tone: させたんです — "I made them do it, you see…" Form: させ + た + んです

Jikan ga nakatta node, isogasetan desu.
時間がなかったので、急がせたんです。
We didn't have time, so I made them hurry, you know.

Nuance: soft explanation, justification, or background.

> Note: 急がせる (isogaseru) has NOTHING to do with 忙しい (isogashii). Although isogu and isogashii look similar in romaji, they are completely unrelated words in Japanese.
> 急ぐ (isogu)
> - Verb
> - **Meaning: to hurry**
> - Base for the causative 急がせる ("to make someone hurry")
>
> 忙しい (isogashii)
> - i-adjective
> - **Meaning: busy**
>
> These two words share no kanji, no meaning, and no grammatical relationship. The similarity is purely phonetic when written in romaji.

8. Polite Forms (for completeness).

- させます — make/let someone do (polite)
- させません — don't allow (polite)
- させました — made/let someone do (polite past)
- させられます — be made to do (polite passive-causative)

Think of させ like the English fragment: "make someone…"
You can't say: "I make someone."
You need:

- "I make someone do it."
- "I made someone go."
- "I won't make someone try."

Same logic in Japanese.

～tachi ～たち:

The suffix ～たち is a plural / group identity marker. ～たち attaches to nouns referring to people, animals, or personified entities to express plurality or group identity. It does not simply mean "plural" in the English sense, it often carries a nuance of collectivity, belonging, or the group associated with X.

It is a structural suffix, not a verb form, which is why it belongs in Part VI: Voice & Agency. What it does:

- It marks people or animate groups.
- It can imply X and their group, not just "X + s."
- It is not used for inanimate objects (you don't say hon-tachi for "books").
- It is often used for polite pluralization (e.g., watashitachi = "we").

Some common forms are:

- watashitachi 私たち → we
- anatatachi あなたたち → you (plural)
- kodomotachi 子どもたち → children
- gakuseitachi 学生たち → students
- senseitachi 先生たち → teachers

Sample Sentences:

1) Kodomotachi wa <u>kōen</u> de **asonde** iru.
子どもたちは<u>公園</u>で**遊んで**いる。
The children are **playing** in the <u>park</u>.
<u>Nuance: たち marks a natural group: "the kids."</u>

2) Watashitachi wa **ashita** kaigi ni demasu.
私たちは**明日**会議に出ます。
We will attend the meeting **tomorrow**.
Nuance: たち pluralizes the speaker politely and naturally.

3) Nihonjin-tachi wa kono **matsuri** o taisetsu ni shite iru.
日本人たちはこの**祭り**を大切にしている。
The Japanese people cherish this **festival**.
Nuance: たち emphasizes the group identity of "Japanese people" as a cultural collective.

Note: shite iru (している) = "are doing / are in the state of doing." In this sentence, している comes from:

- する — to do
- している — to be doing / to be in the state of doing

But the key is this: taisetsu ni suru 大切にする = "to treat something as important / to value / to cherish."
So:

- 大切にしている

literally means:
"are treating (it) as important."

Note: 大切 (taisetsu) is one of those Japanese words that looks like it has two meanings, but in reality it has one core meaning that branches into two natural English translations.

There is one underlying meaning: important in a way that you protect, value, or hold dear. From that core, English splits it into two natural translations: "important" and "cherish / treasure / hold dear."

~たち does not always mean a strict plural. It can mean "X and their group," such as:
Tanaka san tachi 田中さんたち → Tanaka and the people with him
Sensei tachi 先生たち → the teachers (as a group)
It marks who is acting, not just how many.

Kanjiru 感じる:

A transitive verb meaning "to feel," "to sense," or "to perceive" something, either physically or emotionally. It expresses internal experience, subjective perception, or intuitive awareness.

Diving into the core meanings:

1. To feel (emotionally)
   - sadness, joy, fear, gratitude, loneliness, relief, etc.
2. To sense / perceive (physically or intuitively)
   - cold, heat, pain, atmosphere, presence, danger, mood, etc.
3. To find / regard / experience something as X

Often used with 〜to kanjiru 〜と感じる ("to feel that…").

1) Samukute, te ga **kanjinaku** natta.
寒くて、手が感じなくなった。
It was so cold my hands went **numb**.
Nuance: 感じる expresses physical sensation (or loss of it).

> Note: The form 寒くて (samukute) is the te-form of an i-adjective (寒い → 寒くて). For i-adjectives, the te-form is always made by changing: 〜い → 〜くて. This te-form connects the adjective to what follows.
>
> Here, samukute 寒くて expresses:
> - cause ("because it was cold…")
> - linked state ("being cold, [so]…")
> - a natural sequence ("it was cold, and then…")
>
> So the literal structure is:
> 寒くて — "being cold / because it was cold"
> 手が感じなくなった — "my hands became unable to feel"
> Put together:
> "Because it was cold, my hands lost sensation."
> "It was cold, so my hands went numb."

2) Kanojo no **kotoba** ni yasashisa o kanjita.
彼女の言葉に優しさを感じた。
I felt kindness in her **words**.
Nuance: Emotional perception: sensing warmth or intention.

3) Kono **heya** wa sukoshi kurai to kanjiru.
この部屋は少し暗いと感じる。
I feel that this **room** is a little dark.
Nuance: Subjective judgment; the speaker's personal perception.

> Side-note: 暗い (kurai) sounds the same as くらい ("about"). Japanese has many homophones, and くらい is one of the most common. Two completely unrelated words share the exact same pronunciation:

1. 暗い（くらい）— dark
An i-adjective meaning "dark," "dim," or "gloomy."
- Kono heya wa kurai / この部屋は暗い / This room is dark.

2. ～くらい / ～ぐらい — about / approximately
A particle-like suffix meaning "about," "around," or "approximately."
- San-jikan kurai **matta** / 三時間くらい**待った** / I **waited** about three hours."

4) Kare wa **shippai** o osorete iru to kanjiru.
彼は**失敗**を恐れていると感じる。
I feel that he is afraid of **failing**.
Nuance: 感じる introduces an intuitive interpretation of someone else's emotional state.

5) **Shizen** no naka de iru to, kokoro ga ochitsuku to kanjiru.
自然の中でいると、心が落ち着くと感じる。
When I'm in **nature**, I feel that my heart settles.

Nuance: Internal state + personal awareness.

Note: There are two と's in this sentence, and each one plays a different role.

1. The first と — "when / whenever" (natural sequence と). Shizen no naka de iru to (自然の中でいると) literally means: when I am in nature / whenever I am in nature. Here, the structure is: X happens → Y naturally follows. Being in nature → heart settles (naturally).

2. The second と — "that…" (quoting と). Kokoro ga ochitsuku to kanjiru (心が落ち着くと感じる) literally means: I feel that my heart settles.

This と is the quoting と, the same one used with omou 思う, iu 言う, shinjiru 信じる, etc.
It marks the content of the feeling:
- kokoro ga ochitsuku (心が落ち着く) → "my heart settles"
- と → marks this as the internal content
- kanjiru (感じる) → "to feel / to sense / to perceive"

So the structure is:
I feel *that* my heart settles.

PART VII: LISTING AND APPROXIMATION

Key stems and nuances in this section:

- ～tari～tari ～たり～たり gurai ぐらい, kurai くらい, nado など, toka とか, ya や → Expressing non-exhaustive lists and approximation

Vocabulary to review:

bōshi	帽子	hat
budō	ぶどう	grapes
bunpō	文法	grammar
itami	痛み	pain
jibun	自分	myself
kaburu	かぶる	to wear on the head
mada heta	まだ下手	I'm still not skilled yet (direct)
mada mada	まだまだ	still improving (modest)
mikan	みかん	mandarin orange
ongaku	音楽	music
oto	音	sound
sentaku	洗濯	laundry
shinakya	しなきゃ	I have to, I gotta
tango	単語	word
yameru	やめる	stop, quit
yoku	よく	often
zasshi	雑誌	magazine

Diving further into the stems and nuances

～tari～tari ～たり～たり:

This phrase expresses a non-exhaustive list of actions, the same way ya や / nado など / toka とか list nouns. It is the verb-based listing pattern of Japanese, built from the past tense (～た) of each verb plus り, and it always ends with suru する (or a variant like shite iru している / shimashita しました / suru koto ga aru することがある).

～たり～たり lists multiple actions as examples, with the clear nuance that the list is not complete. It often conveys:

- doing things like A and B

- a mix of activities
- alternating actions ("sometimes A, sometimes B")
- a soft, flexible, non-committal tone
- "for example…" but for verbs, not nouns

It is the action-listing counterpart to や and とか.

Each verb takes the past tense (〜た) + り:

- taberu 食べる → tabeta 食べた → tabetari 食べたり
- iku 行く → itta 行った → ittari 行ったり
- yomu 読む → yonda 読んだ → yondari 読んだり
- suru する → shita した → shitari したり

Then the sentence ends with する:
Aたり Bたり する

Polite: Aたり Bたり します
Progressive: Aたり Bたり している
Occasional: Aたり Bたり することがある

Example sentences:

1) **Nichiyōbi** wa eiga o mitari, sanpo <u>shitari</u> suru.
日曜日は映画を見たり、散歩<u>したり</u>する。
On **Sundays** I <u>do things like</u> watch movies and take walks.

Nuance: A relaxed mix of typical activities.

Note: したり is the たり-form of the verb する (to do), used inside the pattern: Aたり Bたり する. But したり does not mean "to do." It means "doing things like…" when used as part of the 〜たり〜たり structure. The り changes the function entirely. It turns the verb into a listed example, not an independent action.

- する = "to do"
- した = "did"
- したり = "do things like… / sometimes do…"

Note: The pairing したり...する looks strange to beginners because it feels like you're saying:

- したり = "doing things like…"
- する = "to do"

So it looks like "doing things like… do."

But in Japanese, these two forms are not duplicates. They play two completely different grammatical roles, and that's why they sit next to each other naturally.
The function of shitari is:
"doing things like…"
"sometimes doing…"
"one example of an action is…"
It is not the main verb of the sentence. The final する is the main verb that completes the entire ～たり～たり structure.

2) **Yasumi no hi** wa netari hon o yondari shimasu.
休みの日は寝たり本を読んだりします。
On my **days off** I sleep, read books, and so on.

Nuance: Non-exhaustive, soft listing of actions.

3) Kanojo wa **warattari** naitari de isogashii.
彼女は**笑ったり**泣いたりで忙しい。
She's busy with all the **laughing** and crying.

Nuance: Alternating emotional actions.

4) **Kodomo-tachi** wa asondari tabetari shite ita.
子どもたちは遊んだり食べたりしていた。
The **kids** were playing, eating, and doing various things.

Nuance: A lively mix of actions.

Comparison with other listing patterns:

Pattern	What it lists	Tone	Example meaning
AたりBたりする	actions	soft, flexible	do things like A and B
AやB	nouns	neutral	A and B and…
AとかBとか	nouns	casual, approximate	things like A or B
AとB	nouns	exact	A and B (complete list)

Gurai ぐらい / Kurai くらい:

These forms have two unrelated meanings: (1) approximation ("about"), which belongs in Part VII, and (2) degree/extent ("to the point that"), which belongs in Part V.

In this section, we are focusing on the approximation meaning of ぐらい / くらい, the one that means "about," "around," or "approximately." This use has nothing to do with intensity or emotional extent. Instead, it simply gives a rough estimate of quantity, time, amount, or number. It attaches directly to nouns, counters, and time expressions to show that the value is not exact. For example:

San-jikan kurai matta.
三時間くらい待った。
I waited about three hours.

Hyaku-nin gurai ita.
百人ぐらいいた。
There were around a hundred people.
These meanings express approximation or rough estimation.

> Note: くらい and ぐらい are interchangeable. ぐらい is slightly more colloquial, but both are used in all contexts.

Kurai くらい: See entry for "Gurai ぐらい / Kurai くらい" above.

Nado など:

A particle used to list examples, soften statements, or mean "and so on / things like…" It can also express modesty or self-deprecation when referring to oneself. Think of など as a gentle way to say "for example," "things like," or "and so on," without sounding rigid or exhaustive.

1) Listing examples ("things like…"):

Kēki ya kukkī nado o **katta**.
ケーキやクッキーなどを**買った**。
I **bought** cake, cookies, and things like that.
Here, など shows that the list is not complete — just examples.

2) Softening statements ("and such things"). など can make a statement feel less absolute or less forceful:

Kare wa manga nado o <u>yoku</u> yonde iru.
彼はマンガなどを<u>よく</u>読んでいる。
He <u>often</u> reads manga and things like that.

This avoids sounding like manga is the only thing he reads.

3) Modesty or self-deprecation ("someone like me…"). When used with watashi 私 / boku 僕 / jibun 自分, など becomes a humble or self-downplaying expression:

Watashi nado, mada mada desu.
私など、まだまだです。
Someone like me still has a long way to go.

Here, など softens the speaker's self-reference, making it humble and polite.

> Note: The literal meaning of **mada mada (まだまだ)** is "still, still". In English, it conveys: "not there yet," "still a long way to go," "still improving," "far from finished." It does **not** simply mean "not good yet." It's broader and more encouraging. Think of it as: "I'm still in progress," "I've got more to learn," "I'm not done growing yet."
>
> A related phrase: まだ下手 (mada heta) does mean "not good yet," but it's more direct and less modestly polite than まだまだ.
> Example:
> Nihongo wa **mada heta** desu.
> 日本語はまだ下手です。
> I'm **still not good** at Japanese.
> This is factual, not self-deprecating.

4) Dismissive nuance ("things like that…"). Depending on tone, など can also express dismissal or downplaying.

Ano **hito** no iu koto nado ki ni shinai.
あの人の言うことなど気にしない。
I don't care about what that **person** says.
This nuance is emotional, but still fits the "approximation / downplaying" logic.

For better comprehension, here is a side-by-side comparison:

Form	Meaning	Example
X など	"things like X / X and so on"	Kēki nado / ケーキなど (things like cake)
X や Y など	listing examples	Kēki ya kukkī nado ケーキやクッキーなど Cakes and cookies, etc.
私など	modesty / "someone like me"	Watashi nado mada mada desu 私などまだまだです I still have a long way to go.

X など…	dismissive / downplaying	Iu koto nado ki ni shinai 言うことなど気にしない I don't care what they say.

Note: など means "things like…" in a modest or softening way. A similar listing word, toka (とか), is coming up next — it's more casual and often used in spoken examples.

Toka とか:

A casual listing marker used mainly in spoken Japanese. It shows non-exhaustive examples, similar to "like…," "such as…," or "things like…." It often carries a soft, approximate, or exploratory tone.

Unlike など (neutral/formal) and や (neutral), とか feels conversational and loose, often implying:

- "for example…"
- "things like…"
- "or something like that…"
- "maybe… / I might…" (when used with verbs)

とか lists examples casually, shows the list is not complete, softens statements, adds an "I'm just giving examples nuance, and can appear after nouns or verbs.

1) Kēki toka kukkī toka **tabetai**.
ケーキとかクッキーとか**食べたい**。
I **want to eat** cake or cookies or something like that.
Nuance: とか shows casual, non-exhaustive examples.

2) **Nichiyōbi** wa eiga toka shōpingu toka suru.
日曜日は映画とかショッピングとかする。
On **Sundays** I do things like watch movies or go shopping.
Nuance: とか lists typical activities without sounding formal or fixed.

3) Ano hito, itsumo **bōshi** toka kabutte iru yo ne.
あの人、いつも**帽子**とかかぶっているよね。
That person is always wearing **hats** and stuff.
Nuance: とか adds a soft, observational tone.

4) **Ashita** wa kaimono toka dekiru to ii na.
明日は買い物とかできるといいな。
I hope I can do some shopping or something **tomorrow**.

Nuance: とか softens the wish, making it sound casual and flexible.

5) Tabako o yameru toka **itte** nakatta?
タバコをやめるとか**言って**なかった?
Didn't you **say** something about quitting smoking?

Nuance: とか marks the content loosely — "something like quitting smoking."

> Note: Yameru (やめる) is one of the Japanese "stop verbs." It means "to stop doing something" or "to quit" (a habit, action, or job). It belongs to a small group of Japanese verbs that all translate as "stop" in English but behave differently in meaning and grammar.
>
> For a full explanation of yameru やめる / tomeru とめる / yamu やむ, including how they differ and how forms like yanda やんだ are conjugated, see the Appendix.

Ya や:

The や form is a neutral, written-friendly listing marker used to connect two or more nouns. It means "X and Y and…" and implies that the list is not complete, but without the casual looseness of とか or the formality of など.

や is perfect when you want to list examples in a calm, matter-of-fact way. What や does:

- Connects nouns only (never verbs or clauses)
- Indicates a non-exhaustive list
- Feels neutral, neither formal nor casual
- Often used in everyday speech and writing
- Implies "among other things," but more subtly than など

1) Hon ya **zasshi** o katta.
本や**雑誌**を買った。
"I bought books and **magazines** (and other things)."

Nuance: や lists items without sounding casual or sloppy.

2) Kyō wa kaimono ya **sentaku** o shinakya.
今日は買い物や**洗濯**をしなきゃ。
"Today I have to do shopping and **laundry** (and more)."
Nuance: や shows typical tasks without implying a complete list.

3) Nihon de wa sushi ya tempura ga **yūmei** da.
日本では寿司や天ぷらが**有名**だ。
"In Japan, sushi and tempura are famous."

Nuance: や gives representative examples in a neutral tone.

4) Kurasu de wa **bunpō** ya tango o benkyō suru.
クラスでは**文法**や単語を勉強する。
"In class we study **grammar**, words, and so on."
Nuance: や is appropriate for academic or descriptive contexts.

> Note: tango たんご（単語） means "word," not "vocabulary." But because vocabulary is made of words, learners sometimes blur the distinction. Japanese keeps them separate. The word for vocabulary (the collection) is goi 語彙.

When listing multiple nouns with や, you repeat や between each item. Just like と and とか, や is a linking particle, so it naturally appears between each listed noun.

1) **Hon** ya zasshi ya shinbun ga aru.
本や雑誌や新聞がある。
There are **books**, magazines, newspapers, and so on.

2) Ringo ya mikan ya **budō** o katta.
りんごやみかんや**ぶどう**を買った。
I bought apples, mandarins, **grapes**, and so on.

3) **Ongaku** ya eiga ya geemu ga suki da.
音楽や映画やゲームが好きだ。
I like **music**, movies, games, and so on.

4) Nihon de wa sushi ya tempura ya udon ga **ninki** da.
日本では寿司や天ぷらやうどんが**人気**だ。
In Japan, sushi, tempura, udon, and so on are **popular**.

や connects nouns only. If you need to list actions, use とか or ～たり～たり instead.

Comparison: など・や・とか — Listing & Approximation

Marker	What It Lists	Nuance	Typical Translation
など	Nouns	"These are examples; the list continues." Clear, structured, slightly formal.	"etc." / "and so on"
や	Nouns	Representative examples in a calm, matter-of-fact tone. Not casual, not formal.	"X and Y and…"
とか	Nouns and Verbs	Soft, approximate. Feels exploratory or offhand.	"like…," "things like…," "or something like that"

PART VIII OTHER IMPORTANT WORDS — NATURAL-SPOKEN JAPANESE

Contractions, reductions, casual fillers, pronunciation shifts, spoken-only variants, and essential connective phrases that appear constantly in real conversation but don't fit into the functional categories above.

Key stems and nuances in this section:

- ～nakya ～なきゃ → contracted conditional form of ～nakereba ～なければ.
- ano あの, e to えと, maa まあ → Fillers
- ittete 行ってて → contraction pattern
- natte なって → te-form of naru, "to become," used to link a change of state to what follows.
- ni tsuite について → topic of discussion.
- no koto のこと → Literally: "the matter of ~ / things about ~."
- okurarete kita 送られて 来た → the process of sending and arriving to imply received.
- sa さ → casual sentence-ending / filler particle.
- teru てる → progressive / habitual / resulting state.
- to iu koto wa と 言う 事 わ→ logical-conclusion connector or inference connector.
- yōna ような → Comparative/descriptive structure ("like ~ / similar to ~")

Vocabulary to review:

bunka	文化	culture
daijōbu	大丈夫	okay, all right, no problem
dōbutsu	動物	animal
deru	出る	to go out / to come out / to appear / to answer (a phone or door)
hada	肌	skin
hanashiau	話し合う	to discuss, to talk something over, to exchange opinions, to deliberate together, to work something out through conversation
jūbun	十分	sufficient
kao	顔	face
katsudō	活動	activity
manabu	学ぶ	to learn about

owaraseru	終わらせる	to make something end, to finish something, to bring something to completion
ronbun	論文	paper, thesis
sakki	さっき	a moment ago, earlier, just now
shinju	真珠	pearl
shōrai	将来	future
shūmatsu	週末	weekend
tanomu	頼む	to request, to ask, to order (at a restaurant), to rely on
tenshi	天使	angel
tsumori	つもり	intention, plan to
yoru	夜	night, evening
yume	夢	dream
yūrei	幽霊	ghost

Diving further into the stems and nuances

～nakya ～なきゃ:

(This is the casual contraction of ～nakereba ～なければ.) A spoken form meaning "if (I) don't…" It is incomplete by itself. When followed by ikenai いけない, it forms the full obligation "I should…" / "I gotta…" / "I must…" For example: Hayaku okinakya ikenai (早く起きなきゃいけない) → I have to wake up early.

In casual speech, however, "～nakya" often ends a sentence and **implies** the missing いけない. The full obligation is still understood.

Example with implied ikenai (いけない)：
Ikanakya.
行かなきゃ。
I gotta go. (I must go.)

(Literally: "If I don't go…" but the implied いけない supplies the obligation.)

Example with full obligation:
Benkyō shinakya ikenai.
勉強しなきゃいけない。
I must study.

Ano あの:

あの is a hesitation filler used when the speaker needs a moment before speaking, wants to soften an interruption, or is searching for the right words. It signals a gentle, socially aware pause, "I'm about to say something, give me a second." It's less about thinking (that's えと) and more about softening the social moment.

What あの expresses:
- A polite hesitation before speaking
- A soft way to get someone's attention
- A buffer before saying something delicate or unexpected
- A moment to gather thoughts while signaling "I'm not done yet"

It's the Japanese equivalent of:
- "Um…"
- "Uh, excuse me…"
- "Well, the thing is…"

But with a slightly more social and polite tone than English fillers.

How it functions in conversation:
あの appears at the start of a sentence when:
- you're about to interrupt
- you need to ask something slightly awkward
- you're searching for words
- you want to soften the impact of what follows

It's a small word, but it carries a lot of emotional intelligence.

Example sentences:
Ano, chotto ii desu ka.
あの、ちょっといいですか。
Um, do you have a moment? [Literally: Um… is a little (of your time) okay?]
(Softens an interruption.)

Ano, sono… **namae** o <u>wasurechatte</u>.
あの、その…**名前**を<u>忘れちゃって</u>。
Um, well… <u>I forgot</u> your **name**.
(Softens an awkward admission.)

> Note: その (sono) keeps its core meaning "that," but in spoken Japanese it also works as a soft hesitation marker; a tiny buffer that lets the speaker ease into what they're about to say. In the example:
> あの、その…名前を忘れちゃって。
> Um, well… I forgot your name.

Here, the その doesn't point to an object ("that thing"). Instead, it functions like:

- "well…"
- "uh, the… you know…"
- "so, um…"

This happens because その can refer not only to physical things but also to the idea you're about to mention. When the speaker hasn't fully formed the idea yet, その becomes a natural "placeholder" for the upcoming thought.

---

e to えと:

This word is the filler people use when they need thinking time. It signals that the speaker is mentally searching for information, recalling something, or planning what to say next. Unlike あの, which softens the social moment, えと softens the cognitive moment with "my brain is loading; hold on."

It appears when the speaker:

- is trying to remember something
- needs a moment to organize thoughts
- is choosing the right word
- is about to correct themselves
- is mentally scanning options

It's the Japanese equivalent of:

- "uh…"
- "um…"
- "let me think…"
- "hmm…"

The tone is neutral and not especially polite or casual. It does not soften interruptions (that's あの). It does not express stance or hedging (that's まあ). It is pure mental processing.

Example sentences:

Eto, ashita no **yotei** wa…
えっと、明日の**予定**は…
Um, tomorrow's **schedule** is…
(Thinking while recalling information.)

Eto… namae wa nan deshita kke?
えと…名前は何でしたっけ?
Uh… what was your name again?
(Searching memory before asking.)

Note: 〜っけ (kke) is a sentence-ending memory-recall marker. It's used when the speaker is trying to remember something and is asking for confirmation. In えと…名前は何でしたっけ？, it softens the question and signals: "What was it again? I'm trying to remember."
Breakdown:

- えと — "uh…" (thinking)
- 名前は — "as for your name…"
- 何でした — "what was it…"
- っけ — "…again? I'm trying to remember."

The nuance is gentle and apologetic, not demanding.
Native speakers use 〜っけ constantly when:

- recalling dates, names, times
- trying to remember instructions
- confirming something they once knew

It's one of the most natural "memory-search" tools in spoken Japanese.

---

ittete 行ってて:

The form 行ってて is a spoken contraction of 行っていて (itte ite), which comes from the verb 行く (iku, "to go"). It does not function as a standalone vocabulary word. Instead, it is a compressed te-form + いる structure used in everyday speech to describe an ongoing action or to connect one action to the next. It is something learners will hear constantly in real conversation.

What 行ってて expresses:
行ってて appears when the speaker wants to express:

- being in the middle of going somewhere
- having gone (and being in that state), and then…
- a background action that explains something else
- a sequence of actions in casual speech

It is the contracted form of:

- itte ite 行っていて → "be going / be in the process of going"
- ittete 行ってて → natural spoken reduction

How it functions in conversation. 行ってて is used to:

- describe what someone was doing at the time
- explain why something else happened
- give instructions in sequence ("go first, then…")
- connect actions smoothly in casual speech

It is common in conversation but rarely written in formal contexts.

Example sentences:
Ittete, ato de **renraku** shite.
行ってて、あとで**連絡**して。
Go ahead and then **contact** me later.
Nuance: Instruction sequence.

Note: Why it feels like "go ahead and then…"
The te-form + いる (→ いて → てて) can express:

- a state ("being in the middle of going"), or
- a sequence ("go and then…")

In instruction sequences, the second meaning is the one that surfaces.
So the speaker is essentially saying:
"Go (do that part), and after that, contact me."
This is why the natural English translation uses "go ahead and then…" even though 行ってて is not literally "go ahead."

Note: あと (ato) is a noun meaning "after / the aftermath."

- It literally means "after" as a thing.
- It must attach to something:

Sonno ato そのあと = "after that"
Shokuji no ato 食事のあと = "after the meal"
By itself, it cannot mean "later" in the general sense.
You cannot say:
✕ Ato, ikimasu あと、行きます (Later, I'll go.)
This sounds incomplete.

あとで (ato de) is an adverbial phrase meaning "later."

- This is the correct form when you mean "later (at some later time)."
- It does not imply immediacy.

Examples:
Ato de ikimasu あとで行きます。= "I'll go later."
Ato de hanashimashou あとで話しましょう。= "Let's talk later."

あと is a noun meaning "after," while あとで is the adverbial form meaning "later." Use あとで whenever you want to say "later" in general.

Sakki konbini ni ittete, **denwa** derarenakatta.
さっきコンビニに行ってて、**電話**出られなかった。
I was on my way to the convenience store earlier, so I couldn't answer the **phone**.

(Background action explaining a result.)

Note: The key is that 出る (deru) has several meanings in Japanese, and "answer the phone" is one of its standard, idiomatic uses. 出る literally means "to exit / to come out / to go out." But in Japanese, it also has several extended meanings that English splits into different verbs.
Here are the major ones:

- to go out / come out

Ie o deru / 家を出る / "leave the house"

- to appear / to be published

Zasshi ni deru / 雑誌に出る / "appear in a magazine"

- to attend / participate

Shiai ni deru / 試合に出る / "participate in a match"

- to answer (a phone or door)

Denwa ni deru / 電話に出る / "answer the phone"
Genkan ni deru / 玄関に出る / "answer the door"
This last one is the one learners don't expect.

行ってて is built from 行く ("to go"), but it does not mean "go" by itself. It is a contracted verb phrase, not a vocabulary item. The meaning depends on context and the action it connects to.

Maa まあ:

A stance-softening filler. It doesn't signal hesitation (like あの) or thinking time (like えと). Instead, it expresses a mild, non-committal attitude toward what you're about to say. It's the spoken equivalent of a shrug: "well…", "I mean…", "it's okay, I guess…" The tone is relaxed, non-confrontational, and slightly hedging.

まあ appears when the speaker wants to:

- avoid sounding too strong or blunt
- soften criticism or disagreement
- show that something is "not bad, not great"
- give a nuanced or middle-ground answer
- reduce emotional intensity

It's a stance marker, not a hesitation marker.

Example sentences:
Maa, iin janai?
まあ、いいんじゃない?
Well, I think it's fine, isn't it?
(Soft, non-committal approval.)

Maa, sonna ni **warukunai** yo.
まあ、そんなに**悪くない**よ。
Well, it's **not** that **bad**.
(Downplaying criticism.)

Maa, dekinakute **mo** daijōbu da yo.
まあ、できなくて**も**大丈夫だよ。
Well, **even if** you can't do it, it's okay.
(Soothing, soft reassurance.)

Note: Learners should also know that も has another very common meaning: "also / too." The key is that Japanese uses the same particle for two different functions, and the meaning depends entirely on the structure it appears in.

In ～なくても, the も adds the meaning "even," creating the concessive pattern "even if (not)." So できなくても (dekinakute mo) means "even if you can't do it."

Natte なって:

なって is the te-form of なる (naru), one of the most fundamental verbs in Japanese. It is not a stem or a vocabulary item on its own. It's a conjugated form used to connect actions, show resulting states, or express changes.

なる means "to become / to turn into / to end up as / to reach a state."
Its te-form なって is used to:

- connect clauses ("become and…")
- show a resulting state ("having become…")
- express a change that leads into another action
- soften statements in casual speech

It is extremely common because なる expresses change, and Japanese uses change-of-state verbs constantly.

Here are the core meanings of なって:
1) Change of state + continuation. なって links a change to what happens next.

Atatakaku **natte**, kimochi ii ne.
あたたかく**なって**、気持ちいいね。
It's **become** warm, and it feels nice.

Nihongo ga **jōzu** ni natte, hanasu no ga tanoshiku natta.
日本語が**上手**になって、話すのが楽しくなった。
My Japanese got **better**, and speaking became fun.
This is the most literal use: "become and…"

> Note: Why の (no) is required in this sentence? Because you cannot attach が directly to a verb. Japanese requires a noun or noun-like unit before a particle like が can attach.
>
> - 話す (hanasu) = a verb
> - 話すの (hanasu no) = "the act of speaking" (a noun-like unit)
>
> So の nominalizes the verb phrase, turning it into something that can function as the subject of the sentence.

2) Resulting state ("having become…") なって can describe a state that has already changed and is now the background for something else.

Kuraku natte kita kara, sorosoro kaerou.
暗くなってきたから、そろそろ帰ろう。
It's getting **dark**, so let's head home.

> Note: そろそろ (sorosoro) is a cue word meaning "it's about time to…" or "we should start…" because a natural moment has arrived.
> It signals that:
>
> - the right time is approaching,
> - the speaker feels a transition is appropriate,
> - an action should begin soon, not immediately but gently.

Shizuka ni natte, min'na shūchū shi-hajimeta.
静かになって、みんな集中し始めた。
It became **quiet**, and everyone started focusing.

3) Softening or casual linking. In conversation, なって can simply connect thoughts without emphasizing the change strongly.

Mā, sō natte mo shikatanai yo.
まあ、そうなっても仕方ないよ。
Well, even if it ends up that way, it can't be helped.

> Note: In this case, the phrase "sō natte" means "if/when it ends up that way," not necessarily that it already happened.

Note: There is no verb in 仕方ない. The structure is:

- 仕方 (shikata) = "way of doing," "method," "means"

(a noun derived from the verb stem of する combined with ～方).

- ない (nai) = the negative adjective meaning "does not exist"

So the literal meaning is: "There is no way (to do it)."
And the natural English meaning is: "It can't be helped." "There's nothing you can do."

Dō natteru no?
どうなってるの?
What's going on? / What's happening?
(literally: "What has it become?")

4) Set expressions with なって.
Some common patterns:

- ～koto ni natte iru ～ことになっている — "it is decided / it is supposed to be that…"
- ～yō ni natte kita ～ようになってきた — "has come to be that…"
- ～ni natte kara ～になってから — "after becoming… / since…"

Examples:
Raishū kara hataraku koto ni natte iru.
来週から働くことになっている。
I'm scheduled to start working **next week**.

Note: Why "koto" is needed in this sentence? こと is required because ～ことになる needs a noun-like phrase. こと turns "to work" (a verb) into "the act of working," allowing the grammar to attach. Another way to see it: the grammar pattern ～ことになる / ～ことになっている (koto ni natte iru) requires a noun-like phrase before に (ni). **It cannot attach directly to a verb**.

Mae yori hayaku okirareru yō ni natte kita.
前より早く起きられるようになってきた。
Literally: I've started being able to wake up earlier than **before**.

Note: What does kita imply in this sentence? The verb kita here is the past form of kuru (base meaning for "to come"), used in the grammar pattern: ～てくる (te kuru). This pattern expresses a change that has been developing up to the present. So in this sentence:

- なってきた = "has come to be," "has gradually become," "has been changing toward this state"

It emphasizes:

- a process, not a sudden shift
- a change that started earlier
- and has reached the present moment

Otona ni natte kara, kōhī ga suki ni natta.
大人になってから、コーヒーが好きになった。
After becoming an **adult**, I started liking coffee.

Some learners confuse なって / なっ because:

- it looks like a "stem" (but isn't)
- it appears in many idiomatic expressions
- なる has a wide semantic range
- English splits "become / get / turn / end up / grow / come to be" into many verbs, but Japanese uses なる for all of them

So なって is extremely common and flexible.

---

ni tsuite について:

The phrase attaches to a noun and turns it into the topic of discussion, analysis, or thought. (Noun + について → "about [noun]) "It is more formal, precise, and explicit than simply using を, and it signals that the following verb (話す, 考える, 調べる, 議論する, etc.) is centered on that topic. It behaves like:

- "about…"
- "regarding…"
- "concerning…"
- "in relation to…"

Some common verbs that pair naturally with ～について

- hanasu 話す (to talk about)
- kangaeru 考える (to think about)
- shiraberu 調べる (to research about/investigate)
- giron suru 議論する (to debate / discuss)
- kaku 書く (to write about)
- manabu 学ぶ (to learn about)

1) Kono **mondai** ni tsuite wa, ato de minna de hanashiaimashō.
この**問題**については、あとでみんなで話し合いましょう。
As for this **issue**, let's discuss it together later.

Nuance: については highlights the topic as something requiring focused attention.

Note: Here 話し合いましょう (hanashiaimashō) is used instead of 話しましょう because the meaning is different.

a) 話す (hanasu) means to speak, to talk, to say words. If you say: 話しましょう → "Let's talk." This simply means "let's have a conversation." It does not imply discussion, exchange of ideas, or working something out.

b) 話し合う (hanashiau) means to discuss, to talk something over, to exchange opinions, to deliberate together, to work something out through conversation. It is a reciprocal verb built from:

- 話す (to talk)
- 合う (to match / to do together)

So 話し合う literally means: "to talk with each other." When you say:
話し合いましょう。
→ "Let's discuss it together."
→ "Let's talk it over."
→ "Let's work this out."
This is the natural choice when the topic is: a problem, an issue, a plan, a decision, something requiring group input. Which is exactly the case in the example sentence.

Note: "Later" is best expressed with ato de (あとで), not ato (あと).
a) あと (ato) means: "after," "the aftermath," "later on." It is a noun, not an adverb. By itself, it cannot function as "later" in a sentence.
Examples of あと as a noun:

- sono ato そのあと → after that
- shokuji no ato 食事のあと → after the meal
- shigoto no ato 仕事のあと → after work

But you cannot say: ✕ あと、話しましょう。 This sounds incomplete or unnatural.

b) あとで (ato de) means: "later," "afterward," "at a later time." This is the correct adverbial form used to express "later" in general.

- ato de ikimasu あとで行きます → I'll go later
- ato de hanashimashou あとで話しましょう → Let's talk later
- ato de kimemashou あとで決めましょう → Let's decide later

2) Watashi wa nihon no **rekishi** ni tsuite jūbun ni shirabete kara, ronbun o kakimashita.
私は日本の**歴史**について十分に調べてから、論文を書きました。
I researched Japanese **history** thoroughly before writing my paper.

Nuance: について clearly marks "Japanese history" as the subject of the research.

---

no koto のこと:

The phrase のこと expresses "the matter of ~ / things about ~ / regarding ~." It turns a noun or pronoun into a broader, more conceptual reference, often covering thoughts, feelings, information, memories, or general aspects of that thing. It is not a stem or a particle by itself—it's a noun (こと) attached to の, forming a phrase that points to "the whole situation or set of things related to X." It is extremely common with people, pronouns, and abstract topics.

The phrase expands a noun into something more abstract or comprehensive. Depending on context, it can mean:

- things about ~
- the matter of ~
- regarding ~
- about (someone/something) in a general sense
- the whole situation involving ~

Examples of nouns that frequently take のこと:

- Watashi no koto / 私のこと / (about me / things about me)
- Kare no koto / 彼のこと / (about him)
- Nihon no koto / 日本のこと / (about Japan)
- Shōrai no koto / 将来のこと / (about the future)
- Shigoto no koto / 仕事のこと / (about work)

Using の alone would sound too narrow or too literal. のこと expands the meaning to "all the things related to X." Compare:

- Nihon no bunka / 日本の文化 = Japanese culture (literal, specific)
- Nihon no koto / 日本のこと = things about Japan (broad, general)

Example sentences:
Watashi no koto, dō **omotteru** no?
私のこと、どう思ってるの?
What do you **think about** me?
(のこと makes "me" broader; my personality, behavior, everything about me.)

Note: どう (dō) does not mean "what" by itself. It also does not mean "what do you…?" by itself. Its core meaning is: "how / in what way / by what manner." Everything else comes from that core idea.

どう asks about the manner, way, or condition of something.

- "How?"
- "In what way?"
- "What's the situation?"
- "How does that work?"

It never directly means "what."

In English, "How do you…?" and "What do you…?" often overlap.
Compare:

- どう思う?

Literally: "In what way do you think (about it)?"
Natural English: "What do you think?"

- Dō shita no? どうしたの?

Literally: "How did it happen?"
Natural English: "What's wrong?"

- Dō iu imi? どういう意味?

Literally: "In what way (is this) meaning?"
Natural English: "What does this mean?"

So English translations sometimes use "what," but the Japanese meaning is still how / in what way.

Note: What omotteru 思ってる literally means--
思う → 思っている → 思ってる
= "is thinking" / "is in a state of thinking"
But English doesn't say:
✕ "What are you thinking about me?"
That sounds like "what thought is in your head right now?"
Japanese 思ってる is broader:

- "What do you think (in general)?"
- "How do you feel about…?"
- "What's your opinion of…?"

So the grammar is the same, but the translation shifts to match natural English.

Why てる works differently with 思う--

思う is a psychological verb, and in Japanese:

- 思っている = "to hold an opinion / to feel / to think (ongoing state)"
- 思う (non-progressive) = "to think (in the moment)" or "I think that…"

So:

私のこと、どう思ってるの?

= "How do you think about me?"

→ natural English: "What do you think about me?"

The てる is still progressive, but it expresses a continuing mental state, not a momentary thought.

There is an entry that dives more into "teru" てる below.

Nihon no koto o motto **shiritai**.

日本のことをもっと**知りたい**。

I **want to know** more about Japan.

(Not just facts, but also culture, people, atmosphere, everything.)

Shōrai no koto o kangaete iru.

将来のことを考えている。

I'm thinking about my **future**.

(General future matters, not one specific event.)

Okurarete kita 送られてきた:

This is a form that beginners constantly encounter but rarely get explained well. It's not a stem, suffix, or a conjugation category, but it's essential for understanding natural Japanese, and beginners always struggle with it. Okurarete 送られて means that something (an email, package, or letter) was sent. What confuses learners is that kita きた (the past tense for kuru 来る, "to come") appears together with okurarete, "sent." Japanese bundles these into one natural idea. English expresses this idea differently by simply saying, "I received an email."

Okurarete kita 送られてきた follows this pattern:

was sent → and came to me → I received it

This phrase combines:

- okurareru 送られる (to be sent)
- ～te kuru ～てくる (to come toward me / to arrive)

Together, they express the natural Japanese idea of receiving something that someone sent.

Examples:

- Mēru ga okurarete kita.
  メールが送られてきた。
  I got an email.

- Nimotsu ga okurarete kita.
  荷物が送られてきた。
  A package arrived (that someone sent).

This pattern is extremely common in natural Japanese and expresses the nuance of something arriving toward the speaker.

Teru てる:

てる is the spoken contraction of ている, the helper-verb construction that marks progressive actions ("is doing"), habitual actions ("does regularly"), and resulting states ("is in the state of having done"). It is not a particle and not a stem.

It often overlaps with English "-ing," but only partially. Its meaning is broader and more precise, and it works with every verb. Because てる expresses three different kinds of ongoing or current states depending on the verb, it cannot be equated with English "-ing" alone.

Examples:

1) tabeteru 食べてる (eating)

Ima, kēki tabeteru kara, ato de hanasō.

今、ケーキ食べてるから、あとで話そう。

I'm eating cake right **now**, so let's talk later.

Note: In this specific sentence, から carries the meaning of "so / because." This is the reason-giving から, not the "after" から.

2) itteru 行ってる (going)

Ima, konbini itteru kara, ato de **denwa** suru ne.

今、コンビニ行ってるから、あとで**電話**するね。

On my way to the convenience store right now, so I'll **call** you later.

3) miteru 見てる (watching)

Ima, eiga miteru kara, **ato de** hanashite mo ii?

今、映画見てるから、**あとで**話してもいい?

I'm watching a movie right now, so can we talk **later**?

4) yonderu has two meanings depending on the kanji. A) 呼んでる to call, to call out, to summon B) 読んでる this kanji implies to read:

Soto de **dareka** ga watashi no koto yonderu yo.
外で**誰か**が私のこと呼んでるよ。
Someone outside is calling me.

> Note: Why not just 私 (watashi)? Because 呼ぶ (yobu) in this meaning (to call someone's name) takes a person as an object, but Japanese prefers a more specific, referential form when the object is me / you / him / her in this emotional or personal sense. What のこと adds…
> 私のこと (watashi no koto) means:
> - "me,"
> - "about me,"
> - "the person that is me,"
> - "my whole self / my identity."
>
> It's the natural, idiomatic way to refer to a person as the target of attention, speech, or emotion. Using just 私 (watashi) here would sound:
> - too bare,
> - slightly unnatural,
> - and not the way Japanese normally expresses "calling me (by name)."

Hon o yonderu.
本を読んでる。
I'm reading a **book**.

> Note: As in English, there are different ways to form a sentence:
> 1) Hon o yonde iru.
> 本を読んでいる。
> I'm reading a book.
> This is the standard, fully correct form.
>
> 2) Hon o yonderu.
> 本を読んでる。
> Same meaning, but casual (ている → てる). This is what most people say in conversation.
>
> 3) Hon yonderu.
> 本読んでる。

Even more natural in speech: drop the particle を. Japanese often omits を when the meaning is obvious.

4) Hon o yonde imasu.
本を読んでいます。
Same meaning, but polite.

5) Hon o yonde orimasu.
本を読んでおります。
Same meaning, but extra polite / humble.

Reminder: Although てる looks like other stems in this book, it is not a lexical stem. It's a phonetic contraction of the helper-verb construction ている. Because of that, it behaves more like other spoken reductions:

- chau ちゃう (from te shimau てしまう)
- teku てく (from te iku ていく)
- te iru ている → teru てる

These are spoken forms, not stems.

---

to iu koto wa ということは:

ということは connects two statements. The phrase always refers back to the previous sentence, and turns it into a "fact." Literally: "As for that fact…" And it introduces a conclusion, inference, or interpretation. Which is why it naturally becomes: "which means…", "so that implies…", "so then…", "in other words…" This is exactly what a logical-conclusion connector does.

Avoid calling it:

- a conjunction (it's not)
- a nominalizer (that's ということ without は)
- a topic marker (は is doing that, but the phrase as a whole is a connector)

Step-by-Step Breakdown:
1. と (to) — the quoting particle.
This と does not mean "and." It means "that…" as in quoting or framing a statement. Think of it as putting quotation marks around an idea.
Example:
「Ame ga furu」 **to** itta.
「雨が降る」と言った。
He said "it will rain."
So と introduces the thing being quoted or referenced.

2. いう (iu) — “to say / to call / to refer to.”
Here, いう doesn’t literally mean “say out loud.”
It means:

- “to call something X”
- “to refer to something as X”
- “to describe something as X”

So という means: “called…” / “that is called…” / “that is described as…”

3. こと (koto) — “thing,” but abstract.
Not a physical object — an event, situation, idea, or fact.
So ということ literally means: “the thing that is called…”, “the fact that…”, “the idea that…” It turns the previous statement into a noun phrase.

4. は (wa) — topic marker
This sets up the next part of the sentence:
“As for that thing…”
“Regarding that idea…”
But in natural English, that becomes:
“Which means…”
“So that implies…”
“So that would mean…”

Example to make it click:
Kare wa konai to **itta**. To iu koto wa, watashitachi dake desu ne.
彼は来ないと言った。ということは、私たちだけですね。
Literal:
He **said** ‘he’s not coming.’ As for that fact, it is only us.

Natural English:
He said he’s not coming. **Which means** it’s just us.
That’s exactly how ということは works. It **summarizes the previous idea** and leads to a **logical conclusion**.

ということ (without は):

You can say ということ without は, but it behaves differently. Without は, the phrase never functions as a connector; it simply nominalizes the clause before it, creating a noun phrase like “the fact that…” or “the idea that….” This is its basic grammatical role.

When は is added, however, the entire phrase becomes a logical-conclusion connector—the familiar "which means…" pattern. So the key distinction is not where ということ appears in the sentence, but whether は follows it.

Examples:
Nihon ni ikitai to iu koto wa hontō desu.
日本に行きたいということは本当です。
The fact that you want to go to Japan is true.
Here, ということ is part of the grammar, not a connector.

Kare ga konai to iu koto o shitte imashita.
彼が来ないということを知っていました。
I knew the fact that he wasn't coming.

Benkyō suru to iu koto wa taisetsu da.
勉強するということは大切だ。
Studying is important.

In all of these, ということ is functioning like:
- "the fact that…"
- "the idea that…"
- "the thing of…"

No は needed unless you want to make it the topic.

So the rule is simple:
✓ to iu koto ということ = grammatical noun-maker ("the fact that…")
✓ to iu koto wa ということは = logical connector ("which means…")

Yōna ような:

The phrase ような (yōna) is a Japanese expression, often appearing as のような (no yōna), that functions like an adjective meaning "like," "similar to," "such as," or "as if." It is used to compare a noun to another noun, describing a resemblance, a type, or a specific kind.

Core Meaning and Usage:
- English Equivalent: Like, similar to, such as, resembling.
- Grammatical Function: It acts as a pre-noun adjectival phrase (rentaishi / 連体詞). It directly modifies a noun that comes *after* it.
- Pattern: [Noun A] + のような + [Noun B] → Noun B that is like Noun A.

Examples:

Tenshi no yōna hito.
天使のような人。
An **angel**-like person / A person like an **angel**.

Yume no yōna hanashi.
夢のような話。
A **dream**-like story.

Shinju *no yōna* hada.
真珠のような肌。
Pearl-like skin / Skin as white as a **pearl**.

ような can describe literal similarity or metaphorical resemblance, depending on context.

Example:
Yūrei no yōna kao.
幽霊のような顔。
A face as if (they were) a **ghost** / **ghost-like** face.

ような modifies nouns; ように (yōni) modifies verbs and adjectives.
(e.g., Tenshi no yō ni utau 天使のように歌う = "to sing like an angel.")

Now that you've worked through all eight parts, the following quizzes provide an opportunity to reinforce what you've learned and to test your grasp of the stems and nuances in context.

TEST YOUR STEM AND NUANCE SKILLS

Part I: Assertion & Emphasis — Quiz (15 Questions)

1.
そんなこと言う________、ひどいよ。
Romaji: Sonna koto iu ________, hidoi yo.
English: It's awful to say something like that.
A. しか (shika)
B. なんて (nante)
C. ほど (hodo)
D. まで (made)

2.
君________信じてるんだよ。
Romaji: Kimi ________ shinjiterun da yo.
English: I believe in you, you know.
A. ばかり (bakari)
B. 部屋 (heya)
C. 休み (yasumi)
D. こそ (koso)

3.
俺________、明日こそがんばる！
Romaji: Ore ________, ashita koso ganbaru!
English: Me? Tomorrow I'll really do my best!
A. さ (sa)
B. ぞ (zo)
C. って (tte)
D. ぜ (ze)

4.
今日の映画、すごくよかった________。
Romaji: Kyō no eiga, sugoku yokatta ________.
English: The movie today was really good, you know.
A. あそぶ (asobu)
B. 声 (koe)
C. なんて (nande)
D. よ (yo)

5.
この景色、ほんとに美しい________。
Romaji: Kono keshiki, honto ni utsukushii ________.
English: This scenery is really beautiful, you know.
A. しか (shika)
B. だけ (dake)
C. まで (made)
D. さ (sa)

6.
行く________！早くしろ！
Romaji: Iku ________! Hayaku shiro!
English: We're going! Hurry up!
A. ぜ (ze)
B. なんて (nante)
C. 頑張る (ganbaru)
D. 服 (fuku)

7.
俺が勝つ________！
Romaji: Ore ga katsu ________!
English: I'm the one who's gonna win!
A. ぞ (zo)
B. ばかり (bakari)
C. 庭 (niwa)
D. なんて (nante)

8.
最近、仕事________で、遊ぶ時間がない。
Romaji: Saikin, shigoto ________ de, asobu jikan ga nai.
English: Lately it's nothing but work, so I have no time to play.
A. ばかり (bakari)
B. 態度 (taido)
C. よ (yo)
D. こそ (koso)

9.
甘いもの________食べてると太るよ。
Romaji: Amai mono ________ tabeteru to futoru yo.
English: If you eat only sweets, you'll gain weight.

A. だけ (dake)
B. なんて (nante)
C. さ (sa)
D. ぜ (ze)

10.
本気________言ってるの?
Romaji: Honki ________ itteru no?
English: Are you seriously saying that?
A. よ (yo)
B. ぞ (zo)
C. なんて (nante)
D. こそ (koso)

11.
俺って、明日は絶対 ________。
Romaji: Orette, ashita wa zettai ________.
English: Me? I definitely won't be late tomorrow.
A. 遅れない (okurenai)
B. さ (sa)
C. よ (yo)
D. だけ (dake)

12.
この部屋、広い________。
Romaji: Kono heya, hiroi ________.
English: This room is pretty spacious, you know.
A. さ (sa)
B. なんて (nante)
C. 大切 (taisetsu)
D. 景色 (keshiki)

13.
勝つ________！負けないぞ！
Romaji: Katsu ________! Makenai zo!
English: I'm gonna win! I won't lose!
A. ぞ (zo)
B. よ (yo)
C. さ (sa)
D. なんて (nante)

14.
俺って、昨日夜道で ________ したよ。
Romaji: Orette, kinō yomichi de ________ shita yo.
English: Me? I got startled on the dark road last night.
A. ばかり (bakari)
B. ぜ (ze)
C. びっくり (bikkuri)
D. こそ (koso)

15.
最近、野菜________食べてる。
Romaji: Saikin, yasai ________ tabeteru.
English: Lately, I'm eating only vegetables.
A. さ (sa)
B. ぞ (zo)
C. だけ (dake)
D. 家族 (kazoku)

Answer Key
1–B
2–D
3–C
4–D
5–D
6–A
7–A
8–A
9–A
10–C
11–A
12–A
13–A
14–C
15–C

Part II: Agreement & Reflection — Quiz (15 Questions)

1.
この部屋、静かだ________。
Romaji: Kono heya, shizuka da ________.
English: This room is quiet, isn't it?

A. ね (ne)
B. なあ (naa)
C. わ (wa)
D. 悲しい (kanashii)

2.
昔の写真を見ると、なんだか________気持ちになる。
Romaji: Mukashi no shashin o miru to, nandaka ________ kimochi ni naru.
English: When I look at old photos, I feel kind of nostalgic.
A. ね (ne)
B. なつかしい (natsukashii)
C. かな (kana)
D. よね (yo ne)

3.
今日は大変だった________。
Romaji: Kyō wa taihen datta ________.
English: Today was rough, you know?
A. かな (kana)
B. よね (yo ne)
C. 迷う (mayou)
D. な (na)

4.
明日、晴れるといい________。
Romaji: Ashita, hareru to ii ________.
English: I hope it's sunny tomorrow.
A. 安全 (anzen)
B. かな (kana)
C. わ (wa)
D. なあ (naa)

5.
これで本当に大丈夫________?
Romaji: Kore de hontō ni daijōbu ________?
English: Is this really okay?
A. かな (kana)
B. な (na)
C. 困る (komaru)
D. 大変 (taihen)

6.
その言葉、ちょっと失礼だ________。
Romaji: Sono kotoba, chotto shitsurei da ________.
English: Those words are a bit rude, you know.

A. 問題 (mondai)
B. <u>痛い (itai)</u>
C. よね (yo ne)
D. わ (wa)

7.
最近、忙しくて困ってる________。
Romaji: Saikin, isogashikute komatteru ________.
English: Lately I've been so busy, it's a problem…

A. かな (kana)
B. 丁寧 (teinei)
C. 有名 (yūmei)
D. な (na)

8.
この________、きれいだね。
Romaji: Kono ________, kirei da ne.
English: This scenery is beautiful, isn't it?

A. かな
B. 景色 (keshiki)
C. わ
D. なあ

9.
________休みたいなあ。
Romaji: ________ yasumitai naa.
English: I really want to rest…

A. かな (kana)
B. ね (ne)
C. ゆっくり (yukkuri)
D. よね (yo ne)

10.
これ、別の問題かもしれない________。
Romaji: Kore, betsu no mondai kamo shirenai ________.
English: This might be a different problem, you know.

A. 悲しい (kanashii)
B. 静か (shizuka)
C. よね (yo ne)
D. かな (kana)

11.
春に________と嬉しくなるね。
Romaji: Haru ni ________ to ureshiku naru ne.
English: I get happy when spring comes.
A. よね (yo ne)
B. なあ (naa)
C. なる (naru)
D. かな (kana)

12.
________になるのは大変だよね。
Romaji: ________ ni naru no wa taihen da yo ne.
English: Becoming famous is tough, you know.
A. なあ (naa)
B. ね (ne)
C. かな (kana)
D. 有名 (yūmei)

13.
どうしたらいいの________?
Romaji: Dō shitara ii no ________?
English: What should I do?
A. 悔しい (kuyashii)
B. なあ (naa)
C. ね (ne)
D. かな (kana)

14.
その________、懐かしいね。
Romaji: Sono ________, natsukashii ne.
English: That story is nostalgic, isn't it?
A. なあ (naa)
B. 話 (hanashi)
C. よね (yo ne)
D. 得意 (tokui)

15.
今日は本当に疲れた________。
Romaji: Kyō wa hontō ni tsukareta ________.
English: I'm really tired today…
A.	なあ (naa)
B.	かな (kana)
C.	悔しい (kuyashii)
D.	昔 (mukashi)

Answer Key
1–A
2–B
3–B
4–D
5–A
6–C
7–D
8–B
9–C
10–C
11–C
12–D
13–D
14–B
15–A

Part III: Questions & Uncertainty — Quiz (15 Questions)

1.
いったい何が起きた________?
Romaji: Ittai nani ga okita ________?
English: What on earth happened?
A.	か (ka)
B.	のか (noka)
C.	いったい (ittai)
D.	かな (kana)

2.
その________は何か?
Romaji: Sono ________ wa nani ka?
English: What does that meaning refer to?

A. 開ける (akeru)

B. のか (noka)

C. かもしれない (kamoshirenai)

D. 意味 (imi)

3.

いったい誰が________か?

Romaji: Ittai dare ga ________ ka?

English: Who on earth decided that?

A. 切符 (kippu)

B. 間に合う (maniau)

C. 決めた (kimeta)

D. かな (kana)

4.

この________は本当に大丈夫か?

Romaji: Kono ________ wa hontō ni daijōbu ka?

English: Is this trip really okay?

A. 切符 (kippu)

B. 旅行 (ryokō)

C. 覚える (oboeru)

D. わ (wa)

5.

いったいどこで________いいか?

Romaji: Ittai doko de ________ ii ka?

English: Where on earth should I look this up?

A. しかし (shikashi)

B. のか (noka)

C. 確かめる (tashikameru)

D. 調べれば (shirabereba)

6.

その________はどこで買えるか?

Romaji: Sono ________ wa doko de kaeru ka?

English: Where can I buy that ticket?

A. 切符 (kippu)

B. 旅行 (ryokō)

C. 意味 (imi)

D. 調べる (shiraberu)

7.

________何を予約したか?

Romaji: ________ nani o yoyaku shita ka?

English: What on earth did you reserve?

A.   予約 (yoyaku)

B.   いったい (ittai)

C.   やる (yaru)

D.   決める (kimeru)

8.

これは本当に________か?

Romaji: Kore wa hontō ni ________ ka?

English: Will this really make it in time?

A.   作る (tsukuru)

B.   間に合う (maniau)

C.   ところが (tokoroga)

D.   よね (yo ne)

9.

いったいどうして________か?

Romaji: Ittai dōshite ________ ka?

English: Why on earth did you open it?

A.   いったい (ittai)

B.   意味 (imi)

C.   旅行 (ryokō)

D.   開けた (aketa)

10.

その話は本当________?

Romaji: Sono hanashi wa hontō ________?

English: Is that story true?

A.   か (ka)

B.   予約 (yoyaku)

C.   作る (tsukuru)

D.   いったい (ittai)

11.

いったい何を________か?

Romaji: Ittai nani o ________ka?

English: What on earth did you make?

A. 作った (tsukutta)
B. いったい (ittai)
C. しかし (shikashi)
D. 意味 (imi)

12.
これは誰が________か?
Romaji: Kore wa dare ga ________ka?
English: Who attached this?
A. 予約 (yoyaku)
B. のか (noka)
C. つけた (tsuketa)
D. やる (yaru)

13.
いったいどこで________か?
Romaji: Ittai doko de ________ka?
English: Where on earth did you learn that?
A. 切符 (kippu)
B. のか (noka)
C. 覚えた (oboeta)
D. かもしれない (kamoshirenai)

14.
これは本当に________か?
Romaji: Kore wa hontō ni ________ka?
English: Did you really check this?
A. つける (tsukeru)
B. 確かめた (tashikameta)
C. ところが (tokoroga)
D. 予約 (yoyaku)

15.
いったい何を________つもりか?
Romaji: Ittai nani o ________ tsumori ka?
English: What on earth are you planning to do?
A. つける (tsukeru)
B. のか (noka)
C. ところが (tokoroga)
D. やる (yaru)

Answer Key
1–A
2–D
3–C
4–B
5–D
6–A
7–B
8–B
9–D
10–A
11–A
12–C
13–C
14–B
15–D

Part IV: Explanatory & Causal — Quiz (15 Questions)

1.
雨________、出かけたくない。
Romaji: Ame ________, dekaketakunai.
English: Because it's raining, I don't want to go out.
A. けど (kedo)
B. から (kara)
C. 暑い (atsui)
D. 駅 (eki)

2.
お腹が空いた________、レストランに行きました。
Romaji: Onaka ga suita ________, resutoran ni ikimashita.
English: I got hungry, so I went to a restaurant.
A. おく (oku)
B. ので (node)
C. こと (koto)
D. 出す (dasu)

3.
忙しい________、手伝ってくれた。
Romaji: Isogashii ________, tetsudatte kureta.
English: Even though he was busy, he helped me.

A. し (shi)
B. 電気 (denki)
C. ので (node)
D. のに (noni)

4.
その説明が下手な________、よく分からなかった。
Romaji: Sono setsumei ga heta na ________, yoku wakaranakatta.
English: Because the explanation was poor, I didn't really understand.
A. 地図 (chizu)
B. わけ (wake)
C. ので (node)
D. ちがう (chigau)

5.
今日は暇________、写真を整理するつもり。
Romaji: Kyō wa hima ________, shashin o seiri suru tsumori.
English: Since I'm free today, I plan to organize my photos.
A. から (kara)
B. 近い (chikai)
C. けど (kedo)
D. 最高 (saikō)

6.
外は寒い________、家の中は温かい。
Romaji: Soto wa samui ________, ie no naka wa atatakai.
English: Outside is cold, but inside the house is warm.
A. の (no)
B. し (shi)
C. 暇 (hima)
D. けれど (keredo)

7.
寒い________、外で運動した。
Romaji: Samui ________, soto de undō shita.
English: Even though it was cold, I exercised outside.
A. 点 (ten)
B. のに (noni)
C. 人生 (jinsei)
D. 子ども (kodomo)

8.
歌が下手な________、歌手になりたいんだって。
Romaji: Uta ga heta na ________, kashu ni naritai ndatte.
English: Despite being bad at singing, he says he wants to be a singer.
A. くせに (kuse ni)
B. おく (oku)
C. 引っ越す (hikkosu)
D. けど (kedo)

9.
その人は真面目だ________、とても面白い。
Romaji: Sono hito wa majime da ________, totemo omoshiroi.
English: He's serious, and very interesting.
A. けど (kedo)
B. し (shi)
C. から (kara)
D. のに (noni)

10.
そんなことを言う________、許せない。
Romaji: Sonna koto o iu ________, yurusenai.
English: I can't forgive you for saying something like that.
A. のに (noni)
B. 安心 (anshin)
C. もの (mono)
D. だって (datte)

11.
彼は働いている________、お金がない。
Romaji: Kare wa hataraite iru ________, okane ga nai.
English: Even though he works, he has no money.
A. から (kara)
B. のに (noni)
C. し (shi)
D. ので (node)

12.
その気持ちは分かる________、やっぱり無理だ。
Romaji: Sono kimochi wa wakaru ________, yappari muri da.
English: I understand the feeling, but it's still impossible.

A. けど (kedo)
B. から (kara)
C. 文句 (monku)
D. だって (datte)

13.
最近忙しい________、練習できなかった。
Romaji: Saikin isogashii ________, renshū dekinakatta.
English: Since I've been busy lately, I couldn't practice.
A. けど (kedo)
B. 着る (kiru)
C. ので (node)
D. し (shi)

14.
そんなに高い________、買えないよ。
Romaji: Sonnani takai ________, kaenai yo.
English: It's so expensive, so I can't buy it.
A. 変わる (kawaru)
B. 仕事 (shigoto)
C. から (kara)
D. 口 (kuchi)

15.
雪が降っていた________、駅まで歩いた。
Romaji: Yuki ga futte ita ________, eki made aruita.
English: Even though it was snowing, I walked to the station.
A. から (kara)
B. のに (noni)
C. ので (node)
D. し (shi)

Answer Key
1–B
2–B
3–D
4–C
5–A
6–D
7–B
8–A

9–B
10–C
11–B
12–A
13–C
14–C
15–B

Part V: Excess & Combination — Quiz (15 Questions)

1.
雨が降った________、公園へ行かない。
Romaji: Ame ga futta ________, kōen e ikanai.
English: If it rains, I won't go to the park.
A. ～たら (～tara)
B. 兄 (ani)
C. そう (sō)
D. まで (made)

2.
この靴は高________買えない。
Romaji: Kono kutsu wa taka________ kaenai.
English: These shoes are too expensive to buy.
A. ～すぎて (～sugite)
B. そうで (sōde)
C. ～たら (～tara)
D. くらい (kurai)

3.
夜________歩き、足が痛くなった。
Romaji: Yoru ________ aruki, ashi ga itaku natta.
English: I walked until night and my feet started hurting.
A. ～すぎて (～sugite)
B. ～たら (～tara)
C. ～なくて (～nakute)
D. まで (made)

4.
彼は美術館が好き________、よく行く。
Romaji: Kare wa bijutsukan ga suki ________, yoku iku.
English: He likes museums, so he often goes.

A. 〜たら (〜tara)
B. なら (nara)
C. 〜がって (〜gatte)
D. ので (node)

5.
もし時間があれ________、散歩しよう。
Romaji: Moshi jikan ga are________, sanpo shiyō.
English: If we have time, let's take a walk.
A. 〜ば (〜ba)
B. 〜たら (〜tara)
C. 休む (yasumu)
D. 〜なくて (〜nakute)

6.
彼女は恥ずかし________、何も言えなかった。
Romaji: Kanojo wa hazukashi________, nani mo ienakatta.
English: She was embarrassed and couldn't say anything.
A. 〜すぎて (〜sugite)
B. 〜たら (〜tara)
C. そうで (sōde)
D. 〜なくて (〜nakute)

7.
財布を落とし________、大変だった。
Romaji: Saifu o otoshi________, taihen datta.
English: I accidentally dropped my wallet — it was awful.
A. 〜ちゃって (〜chatte)
B. 〜すぎて (〜sugite)
C. 〜たら (〜tara)
D. でも (demo)

8.
散歩________、本屋に寄った。
Romaji: Sanpo ________, hon'ya ni yotta.
English: I dropped by a bookstore while taking a walk.
A. 〜たら (〜tara)
B. 〜がてら (〜gatera)
C. 〜すぎて (〜sugite)
D. でも (demo)

9.
連絡し________、心配したよ。
Romaji: Renraku shi________, shinpai shita yo.
English: Because you didn't contact me, I was worried.
A. ～なくて (～nakute)
B. ～すぎて (～sugite)
C. ～たら (～tara)
D. でも (demo)

10.
電車で行く________です。
Romaji: Densha de iku ________ desu.
English: There is no other way but to go by train.
A. も (mo)
B. しかない (shika nai)
C. くらい (kurai)
D. まで (made)

11.
夜ご飯を食べ________、すぐ寝た。
Romaji: Yorugohan o tabe________, sugu neta.
English: After eating dinner, I went straight to sleep.
A. ～たら (～tara)
B. ～すぎて (～sugite)
C. ～なくて (～nakute)
D. でも (demo)

12.
彼は元気________走っている。
Romaji: Kare wa genki________ hashitte iru.
English: He looks energetic as he runs.
A. そうに (sō ni)
B. ～たら (～tara)
C. ～すぎて (～sugite)
D. でも (demo)

13.
買い物________、公園を散歩した。
Romaji: Kaimono ________, kōen o sanpo shita.
English: While shopping, I also took a walk in the park.

A. くらい (kurai)
B. ～がてら (～gatera)
C. でも (demo)
D. ～すぎて (～sugite)

14.
電車が遅れた________、間に合った。
Romaji: Densha ga okureta ________, maniaatta.
English: Even though the train was late, I made it.
A. でも (demo)
B. ～たら (～tara)
C. ～すぎて (～sugite)
D. ～なくて (～nakute)

15.
夜はほとんど人がいない________、静かだ。
Romaji: Yoru wa hotondo hito ga inai ________, shizuka da.
English: At night, there are almost no people, so it's quiet.
A. から (kara)
B. ので (node)
C. し (shi)
D. ～たら (～tara)

Answer Key
1–A
2–A
3–D
4–D
5–A
6–A
7–A
8–B
9–A
10–B
11–A
12–A
13–B
14–A
15–B

Part VI: Voice & Agency — Quiz (15 Questions)

1.
明日、富士山が見________。
Romaji: Ashita, Fujisan ga mi________.
English: I can see Mt. Fuji tomorrow.
A. ～られ (～rare)
B. ～える (～eru)
C. ～たち (～tara)
D. 感じる (kanjiru)

2.
母に叱________ました。
Romaji: Haha ni shika________mashita.
English: I was scolded by my mother.
A. ～ら (～ra)
B. 感じる (kanjiru)
C. ～られ (～rare)
D. 肉 (niku)

3.
子ども________が公園で笑っている。
Romaji: Kodomo________ ga kōen de waratte iru.
English: The children are laughing in the park.

A. 弟 (otōto)
B. ～たち (～tachi)
C. ～える (～eru)
D. ～られ (～rare)

4.
自然の中にいると、心が落ち着くように________。
Romaji: Shizen no naka ni iru to, kokoro ga ochitsuku yō ni ________.
English: When I'm in nature, I feel my heart calming down.

A. 感じる (kanjiru)
B. ～られ (～rare)
C. ～させ (～sase)
D. 落ちる (ochiru)

5.
彼は人を強く押し________ることがある。
Romaji: Kare wa hito o tsuyoku oshi________ru koto ga aru.
English: He sometimes pushes people forcefully.
A. 祭り (matsuri)
B. ～させ (～sase)
C. 飛ぶ (tobu)
D. ～える (～eru)

6.
鳥________が空を飛んでいる。
Romaji: Tori________ ga sora o tonde iru.
English: The birds are flying in the sky.
A. ～たち (～tachi)
B. ～ら (～ra)
C. ～られ (～rare)
D. ～える (～eru)

7.
彼女は上司に会議に出________た。
Romaji: Kanojo wa jōshi ni kaigi ni da________ta.
English: She was made to attend the meeting by her boss.
A. ～る (～ru)
B. 恐れる (osoreru)
C. ～させ (～sase)
D. 踊る (odoru)

8.
この肉はよく焼け________。
Romaji: Kono niku wa yoku yake________.
English: This meat cooks well.
A. ～る (～ru)
B. 立つ (tatsu)
C. 泳ぐ (oyogu)
D. ～たち (～tachi)

9.
彼は自然の美しさを強く________。
Romaji: Kare wa shizen no utsukushisa o tsuyoku ________.
English: He strongly feels the beauty of nature.

A. 感じる (kanjiru)

B. ～られ (～rare)

C. 押し出す (oshidasu)

D. ～たち (～tachi)

10.

弟________は祭りで踊っていた。

Romaji: Otōto________ wa matsuri de odotte ita.

English: My younger brothers were dancing at the festival.

A. ～ら (～ra)

B. ～たち (～tachi)

C. ～える (～eru)

D. ～られ (～rare)

11.

その問題についてもっと________が必要です。

Romaji: Sono mondai ni tsuite motto ________ ga hitsuyou desu.

English: More discussion is needed regarding that issue.

A. 議論 (giron)

B. ～られ (～rare)

C. ～させ (～sase)

D. 残業 (zangyō)

12.

上司に意見を言わ________なかった。

Romaji: Jōshi ni iken o iwa________ nakatta.

English: I couldn't express my opinion to my boss.

A. 恐れる (osoreru)

B. 強く (tsuyoku)

C. ～られ (～rare)

D. ～える (～eru)

13.

彼女はいつも________いる。

Romaji: Kanojo wa itsumo ________ iru.

English: She is always laughing/smiling.

A. ～られ (～rare)

B. 笑って (waratte)

C. ～える (～eru)

D. 歌う (utau)

14.
自然の音がよく聞こえ________る。
Romaji: Shizen no oto ga yoku kikoe________ru.
English: I can hear the sounds of nature clearly.
A. 肉 (niku)
B. ～られ (～rare)
C. 自然 (shizen)
D. ～たち (～tachi)

15.
彼女________は歌が上手だ。
Romaji: Kanojo________ wa uta ga jōzu da.
English: She and her group are good at singing.
A. ～ら (～ra)
B. ～たち (～tachi)
C. ～える (～eru)
D. ～られ (～rare)

Answer Key
1–B
2–C
3–B
4–A
5–B
6–A
7–C
8–A
9–A
10–B
11–A
12–C
13–B
14–B
15–B

Part VII: Listing & Approximation — Quiz (15 Questions)

1.
今日は音楽を聞い________、雑誌を読んだりした。
Romaji: Kyō wa ongaku o kii________, zasshi o yondari shita.
English: Today I listened to music and read magazines and such.

A. たり (tari)
B. とか (toka)
C. 帽子 (bōshi)
D. 音楽 (ongaku)

2.
帽子________かぶって出かけた。
Romaji: Bōshi ________ kabutte dekaketa.
English: I went out wearing a hat and (other things).
A. かぶる (kaburu)
B. 痛み (itami)
C. など (nado)
D. 洗濯 (sentaku)

3.
今日はぶどう________みかんを買った。
Romaji: Kyō wa budō ________ mikan o katta.
English: Today I bought grapes and mandarin oranges.
A. とか (toka)
B. や (ya)
C. 音 (oto)
D. 単語 (tango)

4.
まだまだ練習が必要________だ。
Romaji: Mada mada renshū ga hitsuyō ________ da.
English: I still need about this much practice.
A. たり (tari)
B. くらい (kurai)
C. やめる (yameru)
D. 自分 (jibun)

5.
今日は洗濯________、単語を覚えたりした。
Romaji: Kyō wa sentaku ________, tango o oboetari shita.
English: Today I did laundry and memorized vocabulary and such.
A. とか (toka)
B. ぶどう (budō)
C. しなきゃ (shinakya)
D. 音 (oto)

6.
痛みがひどくて、立つ_______できない。
Romaji: Itami ga hidokute, tatsu ________ dekinai.
English: The pain is so bad I can barely stand.
A. とか (toka)
B. くらい (kurai)
C. や (ya)
D. など (nado)

7.
今日は自分の部屋を片付け_______、音楽を聞いた。
Romaji: Kyō wa jibun no heya o katazuke________, ongaku o kiita.
English: Today I cleaned my room and listened to music.
A. とか (toka)
B. や (ya)
C. など (nado)
D. たり (tari)

8.
みかん_______、ぶどう_______、果物が好きだ。
Romaji: Mikan ________, budō ________, kudamono ga suki da.
English: I like fruits such as mandarins and grapes.
A. とか / とか (toka / toka)
B. ぐらい / くらい (gurai / kurai)
C. など / とか (nado / toka)
D. たり / たり (tari / tari)

9.
今日はまだやめる_______の疲れだ。
Romaji: Kyō wa mada yameru ________ no tsukare da.
English: I'm tired to the point where I feel like quitting.
A. など (nado)
B. くらい (kurai)
C. とか (toka)
D. や (ya)

10.
音_______聞こえたら教えて。
Romaji: Oto ________ kikoetara oshiete.
English: If you hear sounds or anything like that, let me know.

A. 雑誌 (zasshi)
B. や (ya)
C. とか (toka)
D. 洗濯 (sentaku)

11.
今日は泳いだ________、走ったりした。
Romaji: Kyō wa oyoida ________, hashittari shita.
English: Today I swam and ran and did other things.
A. みかん (mikan)
B. かぶる (kaburu)
C. やめる (yameru)
D. たり (tari)

12.
雑誌________読みながら休んだ。
Romaji: Zasshi ________ yominagara yasunda.
English: I rested while reading magazines and such.
A. など (nado)
B. や (ya)
C. 文法 (bunpō)
D. よく (yoku)

13.
今日はぶどう________買いたい。
Romaji: Kyō wa budō ________ kaitai.
English: Today I want to buy grapes or something like that.
A. や (ya)
B. 文法 (bunpō)
C. とか (toka)
D. 自分 (jinbun)

14.
帽子________、服________買わなきゃ。
Romaji: Bōshi ________, fuku ________ kawanakya.
English: I need to buy hats, clothes, and things like that.
A. とか / とか (toka / toka)
B. よく / よく (yoku / yoku)
C. やめる / やめる (yameru / yameru)
D. かぶる / かぶる (kaburu / kaburu)

15.
今日は音楽を聞いたり、雑誌を読んだり________した。
Romaji: Kyō wa ongaku o kiitari, zasshi o yondari ________ shita.
English: Today I listened to music, read magazines, and did various things.
A. とか (toka)
B. 音楽 (ongaku)
C. など (nado)
D. くらい (kurai)

Answer Key
1–A
2–C
3–B
4–B
5–A
6–B
7–D
8–A
9–B
10–C
11–D
12–A
13–C
14–A
15–C

Part VIII: Natural-Spoken Japanese — Quiz (15 Questions)

1.
あの________、ちょっと相談したいことがあるんだけど。
Romaji: Ano ________, chotto sōdan shitai koto ga arun dakedo.
English: Um, I have something I want to discuss…
A. 文化 (bunka)
B. えと (eto)
C. ～なきゃ (～nakya)
D. てる (teru)

2.
夢の________話を聞いた。
Romaji: Yume no ________ hanashi o kiita.
English: I heard a dream-like story.

A. さ (sa)
B. ということは (to iu koto wa)
C. ような (yōna)
D. てる (teru)

3.
さっき送られて________メールを読んだ?
Romaji: Sakki okurarete________ mēru o yonda?
English: Did you read the email that was sent to you earlier?
A. きた (kita)
B. てる (teru)
C. さ (sa)
D. えと (eto)

4.
文化________論文を書いている。
Romaji: Bunka ________ ronbun o kaite iru.
English: I'm writing a paper about culture.
A. 肌 (hada)
B. について (ni tsuite)
C. さ (sa)
D. てる (teru)

5.
最近、夜よく眠れて________。
Romaji: Saikin, yoru yoku nemurete________.
English: Lately, I've been sleeping well at night.
A. さ (sa)
B. てる (teru)
C. ～なきゃ (～nakya)
D. ような (yōna)

6.
まあ________、大丈夫だよ。
Romaji: Mā ________, daijōbu da yo.
English: Well, you know, it's fine.
A. てる (teru)
B. さ (sa)
C. について (ni tsuite)
D. きた (kita)

7.
夜に________、急に寒くなった。
Romaji: Yoru ni ________, kyū ni samuku natta.
English: When it became night, it suddenly got cold.
A. なって (natte)
B. てる (teru)
C. てて (tete)
D. てきた (te kita)

8.
間違ったものが________。
Romaji: Machigatta mono ga ________.
English: The wrong thing was sent to me.
A. てる (teru)
B. 送られてきた (okurarete kita)
C. さ (sa)
D. について (ni tsuite)

9.
その顔、天使の________だね。
Romaji: Sono kao, tenshi no ________ da ne.
English: That face is like an angel's.
A. さ (sa)
B. ような (yōna)
C. てる (teru)
D. について (ni tsuite)

10.
今、ラーメンを食べ________。
Romaji: Ima, rāmen o tabe________.
English: I am eating ramen now.
A. てる (teru)
B. 週末 (shūmatsu)
C. について (ni tsuite)
D. ～なきゃ (～nakya)

11.
夜道を歩くのは怖い________、気をつけてね。
Romaji: Yomichi o aruku no wa kowai________, ki o tsukete ne.
English: Walking on a dark road is scary, so be careful.

A. てる (teru)
B. ということは (to iu koto wa)
C. さ (sa)
D. ような (yōna)

12.
買い物に________、雨が降り始めた。
Romaji: Kaimono ni ________, ame ga furi hajimeta.
English: While I was out shopping, it started to rain.
A. てる (teru)
B. 行ってて (ittete)
C. さ (sa)
D. について (ni tsuite)

13.
夜ご飯を作ら________ないと思ってる。
Romaji: Yorugohan o tsukura________nai to omotteru.
English: I'm thinking I have to make dinner.
A. てる (teru)
B. さ (sa)
C. ～なきゃ (～nakya)
D. きた (kita)

14.
その話、幽霊の________感じがした。
Romaji: Sono hanashi, yūrei no ________ kanji ga shita.
English: That story felt ghost-like.
A. てる (teru)
B. さ (sa)
C. ような (yōna)
D. 学ぶ (manabu)

15.
日本の文化________話しましょう。
Romaji: Nihon no bunka ________ hanashimashou.
English: Let's talk about Japanese culture.
A. てる (teru)
B. について (ni tsuite)
C. さ (sa)
D. きた (kita)

Answer Key

1–B
2–C
3–A
4–B
5–B
6–B
7–A
8–B
9–B
10–A
11–B
12–B
13–C
14–C
15–B

APPENDIX A

WHY JAPANESE HAS TWO "SUBJECT MARKERS" (は and が)

Long before modern Japanese took shape, the language inherited two different grammatical tools from Old Japanese: a topic marker and a subject marker, each serving a distinct role in a sentence. Classical Japanese was a highly flexible, context-driven language where word order carried far less meaning than in English. To keep sentences clear, speakers relied on particles to signal what the sentence was about and who or what was actually doing or experiencing something. Over centuries, these two particles—は (wa) and が (ga)—crystallized into the functions we recognize today. Their coexistence is not redundancy; it's a reflection of how Japanese organizes information: first by theme, then by actor.

The Japanese language uses these two markers to define focus, context, and grammatical roles in a system where word order is fluid. The particle は establishes the topic—the "as for…" element that sets the scene. It does not mark the grammatical subject; it marks what the sentence is about. In contrast, が identifies the subject—the entity that performs an action, experiences a state, or is being identified. In short: は sets the stage; が spotlights the actor within that stage. Understanding this division is one of the most important keys to reading Japanese sentences the way native speakers intuitively do.

Some learners think both は and が are "subject markers because in English, the topic and the subject are usually the same thing. In Japanese, they are separate concepts:

- は = what we're talking about
- が = what does the action / what is being identified

This is why both can appear in the same sentence:

- Watashi wa neko ga suki desu.
  私は猫が好きです。
  As for me, it is cats that I like.

When to use which (the simplest rule that actually works).

Use は when:

- the information is already known
- you're setting the topic
- you're contrasting topics
- you're making general statements

Use が when:

- introducing something new
- identifying or specifying
- expressing what actually performs the action
- describing sensations, abilities, or existence

1) は for information that is already known. (The topic is already established in the conversation.)

Story:
You and a friend have been talking about your trip to Kyoto. The city is already the shared topic.

Kyōto wa, hontō ni **shizuka** deshita.
京都は、ほんとうに**静か**でした。
As for Kyoto, it was really **quiet**.

Why は?
Because "Kyoto" is already known and shared. You're simply adding new information about it.

2) は for setting the topic ("as for…"). (You introduce a new topic you want to talk about.)

Story:
You have given your account of a very exciting weekday trip. Now you're starting a conversation about your weekend plans.

Shūmatsu wa, ie de yukkuri suru tsumori desu.
週末は、家でゆっくりするつもりです。
As for the **weekend**, I plan to relax at home.

Why は?
You're establishing "the weekend" as the theme before giving details.

3) は for contrasting topics. (A vs. B — contrast through parallel は.)

Story:
Sitting in a coffeeshop while enjoying drinks with a co-worker, you're comparing two siblings with very different personalities.

Ani wa **shizuka** desu ga, otōto wa nigiyaka desu.
兄は**静か**ですが、弟はにぎやかです。
My older brother is **quiet**, but my younger brother is lively.

> Side-Note: In this sentence, が is not the subject marker. It is the contrastive connector introduced in Part IV, meaning "but / although / however." When used between two clauses, が creates a soft, neutral contrast. In 兄は静かですが、弟は

にぎやかです, the connector が gently contrasts the two topics marked by は, allowing the sentence to present "A is X, but B is Y" in a natural, balanced way.

Why は?
Using は twice creates a clear contrast:
A は… B は…

4) は for general statements. (Universal truths, habitual facts, or broad categories.)

Story:
At a heavily publicized Cat Convention, you're explaining a general fact about cats before a large crowd.

Neko wa yoru ni katsudō suru dōbutsu desu.
猫は夜に活動する動物です。
Cats are animals that are active at night.

Why は?
は marks "cats" as a general category, not a specific cat.

1) が for introducing something new. (A new piece of information enters the scene.)

Story:
You're walking in a quiet park with a friend. Suddenly, you hear something rustling in the bushes. Your friend hasn't noticed it yet.

Neko ga imasu.
猫がいます。
A cat is here.

Why が?
Because the cat is new information — something the listener wasn't aware of until now. が introduces it into the conversation.

2) が for identifying or specifying ("the one that…"). (Used when clarifying which person/thing you mean.)

Story:
You're at a local favorite bakery with two cakes in front of you. Your friend asks which one you ordered.

Watashi ga **tanonda** no wa, chokorēto kēki desu.

私が**頼んだ**のは、チョコレートケーキです。
The one I **ordered** is the chocolate cake.

Why が?
が marks who performed the action (I did), identifying the correct cake.
This is the classic "the one who…" function.

3) が for expressing what actually performs the action. (Used when emphasizing the true actor or correcting an assumption.)

Story:
A hectic day at work and the deadline for an important report has arrived. Two coworkers are discussing who finished the difficult report. One assumes it was Tanaka.

Tanaka-san **janakute**, watashi ga yarimashita.
田中さん**じゃなくて**、私がやりました。
It wasn't Tanaka — I did it.

> Note: じゃなくて (janakute) is the te-form of じゃない (janai) and means "not A, but B." Because it's a ～くて form, it cannot stand alone. It must connect to what follows, allowing the sentence to continue into the correction or replacement.

Why が?
が highlights the real actor, especially when correcting or emphasizing.

4) が for sensations, abilities, or existence. (Used with feelings, physical sensations, likes/dislikes, and inherent abilities.)

Story:
You and a friend are experiencing a new high-end restaurant. You're eating spicy ramen. Suddenly, your mouth starts burning.

Kuchi ga itai desu.
口が痛いです。
My **mouth** hurts.

Why が?
Sensations and involuntary states naturally take が because they describe what experiences the feeling.

Understanding は and が is more than a grammar point — it's a glimpse into how Japanese speakers shape meaning, perspective, and emotion through structure rather than word order.

These two particles are small, but they carry the architecture of the language on their backs. Once you see how Japanese separates *what we're talking about* from *who or what actually acts or experiences*, the rest of the language begins to unfold with new clarity.

STOP VERBS: やめる vs とめる vs やむ

1. Yameru やめる（止める / 辞める）： to stop an action, habit, or behavior; to quit a job or role. Examples:

Tabaco o yameru.
タバコをやめる。
Quit smoking.

Shigoto o yameru.
仕事を辞める。
Quit a **job**.

Benkyō o yameru.
勉強をやめる。
Stop s**tudying**.
Core idea: Stopping an activity or discontinuing something you're doing.

2. とめる（止める / 留める / 停める）：to stop something physically / to halt. Used when you actively stop something external: movement, actions, people, vehicles, conversations. Examples:

Kuruma o tomeru.
車を止める。
Stop the **car**.

Hito o tomeru.
人を止める。
Stop **someone** (from going).

Sono hanashi wa mō tomeyou.
その話はもう止めよう。
Let's stop that topic now.

Botan de **fuku** o todomeru.
ボタンで**服**を留める。
Fasten **clothes** with a button. (Fixing something in place.)

Core meaning: Bringing something to a halt or preventing it from continuing.

Note: How とどめる (todomeru) is part of とめる (tomeru). Japanese has a family of verbs built from the same core idea: stopping, halting, or fixing something in place.

The base member of this family is:
とめる（止める / 留める / 停める） — to stop / to halt / to fasten. From this core verb, Japanese also has a related, slightly more formal or literary verb: とどめる（留める / 止める） — to keep something in place / to retain / to hold back / to preserve.

Even though とめる and とどめる look different, they share the same root meaning and historically come from the same verb family. The extra ど adds a nuance of:

- holding something in place
- keeping something from moving
- preserving or retaining
- restraining or preventing

So you can think of:
とめる = to stop something
とどめる = to stop it and keep it there / to hold it in place

3. やむ（止む） — to stop (by itself). Used when something naturally stops on its own. Examples:

Ame ga yanda.
雨が止んだ。
The **rain** stopped.

Note: Side-note: Why yanda やんだ is the past tense of yamu やむ (not やまった). The verb やむ（止む） means "to stop" (rain stops, noise stops, pain stops). It is a godan む-verb, so it follows the standard conjugation pattern for む-ending verbs.

Godan む-verbs change like this:

- む → んだ (past)
- む → んで (te-form)

This is the same pattern as:

- yomu 読む → yonda 読んだ (I read it)

- nomu 飲む → nonda 飲んだ (drank)
- sumu 住む → sunda 住んだ (lived)

Why it cannot be やまった.
Learners sometimes expect:

- やむ → やまる → やまった

(because of verbs like 止まる → 止まった)
But that's a different verb:
止まる（とまる）
= to stop intransitively (a car stops, a machine stops)
止む（やむ）
= something ceases (rain, noise, pain)
They are unrelated verbs with different readings, different meanings, and different conjugation classes.
So:

- 止まる → 止まった
- 止む → やんだ

Two different verbs, two different conjugations.

Oto ga yanda.
音が止んだ。
The **sound** stopped.

Itami ga yamuto ī ne.
痛みが止むといいね。
I hope the **pain** stops.

Core meaning: Something ends naturally without someone causing it.

Final Comparison Chart

Verb	Transitivity	Meaning	Typical Use
やめる	Transitive	Stop doing / quit	habits, actions, jobs
とめる	Transitive	Stop something physically / halt	cars, people, conversations
やむ	Intransitive	Something stops on its own	rain, noise, pain

If this appendix has given you even a small moment of "Ah, now I see it," then it has done its job. You now hold one of the most important distinctions in Japanese; a distinction that quietly supports countless sentences, conversations, and expressions of thought.

APPENDIX B — DEEP VOCABULARY & NUANCE NOTES

This appendix presents a small set of vocabulary explanations drawn from the sample sentences in the book. Each entry explores nuance, usage, and related grammar in depth, showing how a single word can open the door to broader patterns in Japanese. These notes are not a complete list of all vocabulary in the book; rather, they serve as models for how learners can analyze new words on their own and uncover the layers of meaning behind them.

Example sentences using new vocabulary words:

amai 甘い:

Part of speech: い-adjective (形容詞 / keiyōshi).
Meaning: sweet (taste), naively easy / lenient (metaphorical), and soft / indulgent (toward someone).

Examples of nuance:
Amai kēki — 甘いケーキ — sweet cake
Kangae ga amai — 考えが甘い — naïve thinking
Chichi wa musume ni amai — 父は娘に甘い — the father is indulgent toward his daughter

What is an い-adjective?

- They end in 〜い in dictionary form
- They conjugate by changing the final い
- They can directly modify nouns
- They can become adverbs with 〜く (amaku, 甘く)
- They can take past, negative, and polite forms

1. Sweet (taste)

Kono kēki, **omotta** yori amai ne.
このケーキ、思ったより甘いね。
This cake is sweeter than I **expected.**

2. Lenient / naïve (judgment, thinking)

Kare no **keikaku** wa amai to omou.
彼の計画は甘いと思う。
I think his **plan** is too naïve.
Here, 甘い means "optimistic to the point of being unrealistic."

3. Soft / indulgent toward someone

Sensei wa kare ni dake amai ki ga suru.
先生は彼にだけ甘い気がする。
I feel like the **teacher** is soft only toward him.

This version shows 甘い used to describe uneven leniency.

---

asobu あそぶ:

Part of speech: verb (五段動詞 / u-verb)
Meaning: to play; to hang out; to have fun; to spend time socially.
Core idea: あそぶ does not mean "to play a game" in the narrow English sense. It's broader. It means to engage in enjoyable, non-work activity, including:

- children playing
- adults hanging out
- going out socially
- relaxing or having fun

It's one of the most flexible "play" verbs in Japanese.

The kanji for asobu is 遊ぶ, though in modern Japanese it's very common to see it written in hiragana. Because "play" is such a basic, everyday concept, Japanese tends to prefer the softer, more approachable hiragana spelling.

Sample Sentences

1. Kodomotachi wa **kōen** de asobu.
子どもたちは**公園**であそぶ。
The children play at the **park.**
→ Basic, literal "play."

～たち (tachi) is a suffix added after a person-related noun or pronoun to show a group. It's often translated as "-s," but it's not a strict plural like English. It simply means "and the others," "and company," "and the group." [～たち (tachi) is covered in Section VI]

Usually used with people (not objects). Beginners often try to say things like:
✗ 本たち (books)
✗ 机たち (desks)
These sound unnatural.
たち is mainly for:

- people

- animals (sometimes)
- characters with personality (in stories)

Example:
Inu-tachi ga **hashitte** iru.
犬たちが**走って**いる。
The dogs are **running**.
(acceptable because animals can be treated like "characters")

In the sentence 犬たちが走っている, the いる (iru) is not the verb "to exist" (いる = to be alive). Here, it's functioning as a helper verb that attaches to the て-form of another verb. It expresses progressive aspect, an action that is ongoing right now.

The dogs are running.
(literally: "The dogs are in the state of running.")
So いる is marking:

- continuous action
- ongoing motion
- right now

It's the Japanese equivalent of English "-ing," but with a nuance of state + action.

2. **Ashita**, tomodachi to asobimasu.
明日、友だちとあそびます。
Tomorrow I'm going to hang out with a friend.
→ Shows the polite form and the "hang out" meaning adults use.

3. Yasumi no hi wa gēmu de asobu koto ga ōi.
休みの日はゲームであそぶことが多い。
On my days off, I often play games.
→ Demonstrates あそぶ with a specific activity (games), and shows how it pairs naturally with で.

Note: Here, こと (koto) is acting like もの (mono) in the sense that both are nominalizers that can mean "thing." But they don't behave the same way, and the nuance is different. こと means an abstract thing, while もの means a concrete or conceptualized thing.

こと (koto) is used for: actions, experiences, general facts, habits, rules, abstract ideas.

Examples:

- Nihongo o **benkyō suru** koto wa tanoshī.
  日本語を**勉強する**ことは楽しい。
  Studying Japanese is fun.
- Gēmu de asobu koto ga ōi.
  ゲームであそぶことが多い。
  I often play games.

(→ "There are many instances of playing games.")
Here, こと is turning the activity into a general concept.

もの (mono) is used for: physical things, specific events, conceptualized "things," reflective or narrative tone.

Examples:

- Katta mono.
  買ったもの。
  the thing he/she/I bought
- Doko de katta mono darou.
  どこで勝ったものだろう。

I wonder about that win — where did it happen?
Here, もの makes the event feel like a specific, graspable thing.

---

bakari ばかり:

Part of speech: A "secondary particle" (fuku-joshi / 副助詞/ ふくじょし).
Core idea: attaches to nouns, verbs, or entire phrases to add nuance. It is not a verb, noun, or adjective. It expresses meanings such as: only, just, nothing but, approximately, about (in some contexts), and just did / just finished doing (with ～ta bakari ～たばかり).

What is a "secondary particle"?
A secondary particle adds extra meaning to a word or phrase without changing the basic grammar structure of the sentence.
Think of it as a nuance-layering modifier placed on top of something that is already grammatically complete. Secondary particles do not mark:

- the subject
- the object
- the direction
- the location

Those roles belong to primary particles such as が, を, に, へ, で.
Instead, secondary particles add shades of meaning like:

- "only"

- "even"
- "about"
- "just"

They sit on top of the sentence's structure, not inside it.

Sample sentences:

- Terebi o **mite** bakari iru.
  テレビを見てばかりいる。
  He does nothing but **watch** TV.

  Here, 見る (miru) is in the て-form, and adding いる marks an ongoing or habitual action — similar to adding "-ing" in English. Without いる, you would have テレビを見るばかり, which is grammatically correct but feels like a fragment ("only watching TV"). With いる, it becomes a full sentence describing a continuous state: "is always just watching TV."

- Amai mono bakari **tabete** iru.
  甘いものばかり**食べて**いる。
  They do nothing but **eat** sweets.

  Here, ばかり follows the noun amai mono 甘いもの ("sweet things"). This shows that ばかり can attach to different parts of a sentence depending on what you want to emphasize:

  Terebi o mite bakari iru
  テレビを見てばかりいる → ばかり modifies the action ("only watching")

  Amai mono bakari tabete iru.
  甘いものばかり食べている。 → ばかり modifies the object ("only sweets")

- Kare wa **shigoto** no koto o kangaete bakari ite, kazoku to no jikan o taisetsu ni shinai.
  彼は**仕事**のことを考えてばかりいて、家族との時間を大切にしない。
  He is always just thinking about **work** and doesn't value time with his family.

  "No koto" のこと means "things concerning ~". In this case, it means "things concerning work." のこと will be covered fully in Section 8.

  Here, ばかり emphasizes the action of thinking (kangaete 考えて).

This sentence has two clauses. To connect them smoothly, いる (to be) becomes its て-form → いて。This allows the sentence to continue into the next clause.

The particle と (to) after kazoku 家族 means "with." It will be covered in depth in Section 5.

---

bikkuri びっくり:

Part of speech: Depending on the sentence, it can function as a noun, part of the suru-verb びっくりする, or an adverbial form (びっくりして = "surprised, startled, suddenly")
Core Meaning: It expresses a sudden emotional reaction — usually mild to moderate surprise, not extreme shock.

1) As a NOUN: a surprise, a startled feeling.

Sono **hanashi** ni wa hontō ni bikkuri datta.
その**話**には本当にびっくりだった。
That **story** was really a surprise.

2) As a SURU-VERB (びっくりする): "to be surprised," "to get startled."

Kyū ni namae o yobarete, bikkuri shita.
急に名前を呼ばれて、びっくりした。
I was **suddenly** called by name and got startled.

- びっくりした = past tense of びっくりする.

3) As an ADVERBIAL FORM (びっくりして): "surprised, startled, suddenly" modifying the action.

Bikkuri shite, **koppu** o otoshisō ni natta.
びっくりして、**コップ**を落としそうになった。
Startled, I almost dropped the **cup.**

Note: Since this example uses 落としそう ("about to drop"), here is a brief explanation of the そう construction that appears inside the sentence.

For the word otoshisō 落としそう, "そう" = "on the verge of ___." So "そう" alone describes a state. While "なる" describes the moment you enter that state.

～そうになる = "to come to be on the verge of ___." This adds なる, which means: to become, to come to be, to enter a state. So:
Otoshisō ni naru / 落としそう になる
= "to become about to drop it"
= "to end up on the verge of dropping it"
= "to almost drop it"
This is dynamic, not static. It answers: What happened?
→ "I came to be in a state where I was about to drop it."

The stem ~そう is covered in detail in Part V: Excess & Combination.

---

hareru 晴れる:

Part of speech: verb (一段動詞 / ru-verb)
Core idea: はれる means "to clear up," most commonly referring to weather becoming clear, bright, or sunny. It can also describe clouds, fog, or mood lifting.

1) Weather clears up:

Gogo ni wa sora ga hareru deshō.
午後には空がはれるでしょう。
The sky will probably clear up in the **afternoon.**

Deshou (でしょう) expresses probability, expectation, or soft confirmation. It means things like:
- "probably"
- "I think…"
- "It will likely…"
- "right?" (soft confirmation)
- "wouldn't you say?"

It's a softener. It makes statements less direct and more polite.

2) Mood or feelings brighten:

Hanashitara kimochi ga harete **kita.**
話したら気持ちがはれてきた。
After talking, my feelings **started to** clear up.

Note: ～tara (～たら) means "when/after" for completed actions, and "if" for hypothetical ones. Context decides which one. In 話したら気持ちがはれてきた, it clearly means "after talking." たら is discussed fully in Section V.

3) Fog clears:

Asa ni naru to **kiri** ga hareru.
朝になると**霧**がはれる。
When morning comes, the **fog** clears.

But 晴れる is never used for physical symptoms improving (clearing up), such as: acne clearing, a rash going away, swelling going down, bruises fading, or a wound healing. Those require different verbs.

For physical conditions improving, Japanese uses verbs like:

- naoru / 治る / to heal, to get better
- hiku / 引く / to subside (swelling, inflammation)
- kieru / 消える / to disappear (marks, spots)

So you would say:

- Nikibi ga naotta.
  ニキビが治った。
  My acne cleared up / healed.
- Nikibi ga hiite kita.
  ニキビが引いてきた。
  My acne is starting to go down.
  Literally: My acne has started to pull back
- Nikibi no ato ga kieta.
  ニキビの跡が消えた。
  The acne marks disappeared.

---

hashiru 走る:

Part of speech: Verb (Godan / u-verb)
Core meaning: to run; to move quickly on foot.

Kanojo wa mainichi **kōen** o hashiru.
彼女は毎日**公園**を走る。
She runs in the **park** every day.

---

iru 要る:

Part of speech: Verb (Godan / u-verb)
Core meaning: to need / to require

> Note: This iru is completely different from いる (iru) meaning "to exist (living things)." Different kanji, different meaning, different verb class.

<u>Kuruma</u> o kau ni wa, **okane** ga iru.
<u>車</u>を買うには、**お金**が要る。
To buy a <u>car</u>, I need **money**.

There is a word (hitsuyō / 必要) that feels similar in English but behaves very differently in Japanese. Both relate to the idea of "needing," but they belong to different parts of speech and follow different patterns. 必要 is a noun (or a na-adjective) meaning "necessary." For example:
Mizu ga hitsuyō da. / 水が必要だ。 / Water is necessary.

Iru いる:

Part of speech: Ichidan verb (ru-verb)
Core meaning: to exist / to be (for living things)

いる is used only for living, animate beings such as people, animals, and sometimes personified characters. For non-living things, Japanese uses ある (aru) instead.

Uchi no <u>niwa</u> ni **chairo** no neko ga iru.
うちの<u>庭</u>に**茶色**の猫がいる。
There is a **brown** cat in my <u>backyard</u> (<u>garden</u>).

NOTE 1: In everyday Japanese, にわ covers: front yard, backyard, side yard, garden area, or general outdoor space around a home. Japanese doesn't usually distinguish "front yard" vs. "backyard" unless the distinction is important.

うらにわ (uraniwa) implies back garden / backyard. It is less common in everyday speech. You use uraniwa only when you specifically want to emphasize "the back side," or the distinction matters (e.g., "not the front yard — the back yard"). Otherwise, it sounds a bit marked or overly specific.

Example where it does make sense:

Uraniwa ni dareka iru.
うらにわにだれかいる。
There's someone in the backyard.
(= important that it's the back of the house)

NOTE 2: In Japanese, うちの (uchi no) literally means "my/our home's…", but in everyday speech it's used much more broadly. It doesn't just mark ownership — it expresses belonging, connection, and personal closeness.

For beginners, think of **uchi no** as: "the ___ that belongs to my household / my family / my place."

This is why Japanese speakers naturally say:

- Uchi no niwa / うちの庭 / our yard, our garden
- Uchi no inu / うちの犬 / our dog
- Uchi no neko / うちの猫 / our cat
- Uchi no ko / うちの子 / our child
- Uchi no kaisha / うちの会社 / the company I work for
- Uchi no gakkō / うちの学校 / my school

It's not bragging or possessive — it's simply how Japanese marks something as part of your "circle." Japanese culture tends to emphasize groups, belonging, and in-groups. So instead of saying "my dog" in a strictly personal sense, the language naturally frames it as: "the dog of my household." This feels warm, natural, and humble. うちの marks something as part of your "in-group," not just something you own.

Isogashii 忙しい:

Part of speech: い-adjective (形容詞)
Meaning: Busy; occupied; having a lot to do.

In Japanese culture, saying 忙しい can sometimes serves as a polite excuse or soft refusal:

Sumimasen ima chotto isogashikute.
すみません 今ちょっと忙しくて。
Sorry, I'm a bit busy right now…

This statement may imply "I can't (or don't want to) talk right now," without being blunt.

In some contexts, isogashii can imply more than just a packed schedule – it can suggest:

- Mental busyness: being distracted or unable to focus.
  Kokoro ga isogashii / 心 が 忙しい / A restless heart or mind.
- Social unavailability: being too caught up to engage with others.
  Isogashi**kute** aenai / 忙しくて 会えない / Too busy to meet

The verb for meet is au 会う.

Why use **kute** (くて)? There are three reasons:

- Connecting adjectives together
  Isogashikute **tsukarete** iru.
  忙しくて**疲れて**いる。
  "Busy and **tired**."
- Showing cause or reason
  Isogashikute ikenai.
  忙しくて行けない。
  I'm busy, so I can't go.
- Softening tone
  Instead of bluntly saying isogashī kara
  忙しいから (because I'm busy), using 忙しくて
  can sound gentler, especially in spoken Japanese.

---

kangaeru 考える:

Part of speech: Ichidan verb (ru-verb)
Core meaning: to think / to consider / to reflect
考える is used when you think deeply, logically, or deliberately about something. (It's different from 思う omou, which is more like "to feel / to have an opinion.")

Kono **mondai** ni tsuite sukoshi kangaete mitai.
この**問題**について少し考えてみたい。
I want to try thinking about this **problem** a little.
English translation: I want to think about this problem a little.

Here, mitai (みたい) is not the "looks like / seems like" みたい (as in neko mitai = "like a cat"). This is a completely different grammar pattern. This みたい comes from 〜てみる (te miru), which means: to try doing something and see what happens. It expresses attempt, experiment, or giving something a try.

Form	Meaning	Example
～てみる	try doing	Tabete miru 食べてみる (try eating it)
～てみたい	want to try doing	Tabete mitai 食べてみたい (I want to try eating it)
Noun + みたい	looks like / seems like / resembles	Neko mitai 猫みたい (like a cat)

---

ki 気:

Part of speech: abstract noun.

Core meanings: 気 is an abstract, multi-purpose noun referring to internal states, mental focus, emotional energy, or intention. Its meaning shifts depending on the expression it appears in, but the underlying idea is always connected to the mind, feelings, or inner state.

1. Underlying idea: mind / feelings / emotional state → Ki ga omoi (気が重い)

Ashita no **kaigi** o <u>kangaeru</u> to ki ga omoi.
明日の**会議**を<u>考える</u>と気が重い。
I feel weighed down when I <u>think</u> about tomorrow's **meeting**.

Meaning: emotional heaviness, reluctance. 気が重い often implies a sense of emotional dread about an upcoming obligation (like a meeting, task, or responsibility).

2. Underlying idea: attention / focus → Ki o tsukeru (気をつける)

Yomichi o aruku toki wa ki o tsukete ne.
夜道を歩くときは気をつけてね。
Be careful when walking at night. Or, Be careful when walking **a dark road**.

Meaning: direct your attention toward safety. 気をつけて is also used as a farewell expression ("Take care").

> Note: In つけて (tsukete), the u in tsu is not silent, but it becomes very weak in natural speech. Japanese often reduces the vowel u after consonants like t, s, and k, so tsukete may sound like "ts'kete," but the vowel is still present.

3. Underlying idea: interest / curiosity → Ki ni naru (気になる)

Ano **eiga**, chotto ki ni naru.
あの映画、ちょっと気になる。
I'm kind of curious about that **movie**.

Meaning: something occupies your thoughts; you can't ignore it.

4. Underlying idea: motivation / willingness → Ki ga susumu (気が進む)

Kyō wa **gaishutsu** suru ki ga susumanai.
今日は外出する気が進まない。
I don't really feel like **going out** today.

Meaning: lacking motivation or feeling reluctant.

> Note: The negative form **気が進まない** means "to not feel like doing something."

5. Underlying idea: mood / temperament → Ki ga mijikai (気が短い)

Kare wa ki ga **mijikai** kara, amari karakawanai hō ga ii.
彼は気が短いから、あまりからかわないほうがいい。
He has a **short** temper, so you shouldn't tease him too much.

Meaning: personality trait (short-tempered).

> Note: Hō ga ii (ほうがいい) is a phrase that means "you should..." (with a positive verb) or "you shouldn't…" / "it's better not to…" (with a negative verb).

6. Underlying idea: spirit / energy / vitality → genki (元気) → fine

Saikin, genki ga nai ne.
最近、元気がないね。
You haven't been looking well **lately**.

Meaning: physical or emotional vitality.

7. Underlying idea: intention / plan → Ki ga aru (気がある)

Kare wa **honki** de ryūgaku suru ki ga aru rashii.

彼は**本気**で留学する気があるらしい。
It seems he **genuinely** intends to study abroad.

Meaning: having the intention or will to do something.

> Note: 気がある can also mean "to be romantically interested."
> Kare wa **kimi ni** ki ga aru to omou yo.
> 彼は**君に**気があると思うよ。
> I think he's **into you**.
>
> The structure is:
> - 気がある = to have interest / to have feelings
> - 君に (kimi ni) = toward you
>
> Put together, the natural English meaning is: "to be into you," "to have a crush on you," "to be romantically interested in you." So the literal meaning is "there is interest toward you," but the natural meaning is "he's into you."

8. Underlying idea: awareness / realization → Ki ga tsuku (気がつく)

Saifu o otoshita koto ni ki ga tsukanakatta.
財布を落としたことに気がつかなかった。
I didn't realize I had dropped my **wallet**.

Meaning: becoming aware of something.

> Note: "To realize / to notice" only happens when つく is inside the expression 気がつく. Tsuku by itself NEVER means "to realize." Without 気が, the verb つく defaults to its other meanings; to stick, to attach, to be affixed, to turn on (lights, appliances), to acquire (a habit, smell, name).
>
> In addition, 気がつく (ki ga tsuku) and 気づく (kizuku) are both correct variations of the same verb meaning "to notice." Note that the が sound drops entirely when using the shortened verb 気づく.

9. Underlying idea: preference / taste → Ki ni iru (気に入る)

Kono mise no kōhī, sugoku ki ni itta.
この店のコーヒー、すごく気に入った。
I really liked the coffee at this place.

Meaning: something suits your taste. 気に入る describes the **moment** something becomes pleasing.

10. Underlying idea: composure / calm → Ki o torinaosu (気を取り直す).

Shippai shita kedo, ki o torinaoshite **mō ichido** yatte miru.
失敗したけど、気を取り直して**もう一度**やってみる。
I failed, but I'll pull myself together and try **again**.
Meaning: regain emotional balance.

> Note: The 〜てみる pattern is NOT "see." It's a separate grammar meaning "try doing." Even though みる is the same verb as "to see," when it appears after a te-form, it becomes a grammar pattern:
> V-て + みる = try doing (something) and see what happens
> So in:
> やってみる (yatte miru)
> = "try doing it"
> = "give it a try"
> The みる no longer means "to see with your eyes."
> It means "to test something and observe the result."

11. Underlying idea: to worry about / to care about → ki ni suru (気にする).

Sonna koto ki ni shinaide. (Used in its negative form)
そんなこと気にしないで。
Don't worry about that. Or, don't let that bother you.
Meaning: to mentally dwell on something; to be bothered by something.

---

natsukashī 懐かしい:

Part of speech: い-adjective (形容詞)
Meaning: nostalgic, memories
Core idea: なつかしい expresses a warm, emotional feeling when something reminds you of the past, a mix of nostalgia, fond memories, and "I remember this… it feels good to think about it." It does not mean "I miss you" in the direct English sense. It means "this brings back good memories" or "this feels nostalgic."

Sample sentence:
Mukashi no gēmu o miru to, natsukashii **na.**
昔のゲームを見ると、なつかしいな。
When I see old games, **ah**, it's nostalgic.

Note: Na (な) here is a sentence-ending particle expressing emotion. This な is not the な from な-adjectives. It's a sentence-ending particle that adds:

- emotion
- personal feeling
- a soft exclamation
- a reflective, inward tone

It's similar to saying:

- "Ah, nostalgic."
- "Wow, that brings back memories."
- "Man… nostalgic."
- "That really takes me back."

It's not strong like yo (よ) or ne (ね). It's more internal, like you're talking to yourself or softly expressing a feeling.

Note: To (と) is the automatic-result conditional. It means:

- "when…"
- "whenever…"
- "if (whenever this condition happens, the result naturally follows)"

It describes a trigger → automatic reaction relationship. So the structure is: A と B. When A happens, B naturally follows.

---

shinjiru 信じる:

Part of speech: Ichidan verb (ru-verb)
Core meanings: to believe (someone or something is true), to trust (have faith in a person), or to have faith / religious belief (contextual). These meanings all come from the same core idea: accepting something as true or reliable.

1) Sample sentence (core meaning: believe)
Kare no **kotoba** o shinjite iru.
彼の言葉を信じている。
I believe what he says (**words**).

This is the most common, everyday use.

2) Sample sentence: trust (a person)
Watashi wa **kimi** o shinjiteru yo.
私は君を信じてるよ。
I trust **you**.
Same verb, but now directed at a person rather than information. (Note: 信じてる is the natural spoken contraction of 信じている.)

3) Sample sentence: religious belief / faith:
Kami o shinjiru hito ga **ōi**.
神を信じる人が**多い**。
There are **many** people who believe in God.

This is still the same verb, just applied to spiritual belief.

NOTE: shinjiru 信じる vs. shinyō suru 信用する. Even though both verbs can translate as "to trust" in English, Japanese draws a clear line between them. While 信じる means believe / trust emotionally, shinyō suru 信用する trusts someone's reliability, competence, or track record. Examples:

信じる (shinjiru)
Nuance: personal belief, faith, or confidence in someone's honesty or words
- Shinji teru yo / 信じてるよ / I believe you.
- Kare no kotoba o shinjiru / 彼の言葉を信じる / I believe what he says.

信用する (shinyō suru)
Nuance: trusting someone's reliability, competence, or track record
- Kare wa shin'yō dekiru hito da.
  彼は信用できる人だ。
  He's a reliable person.
- Kono kaisha wa shin'yō sarete iru.
  この会社は信用されている。
  This company is trusted.

NOTE: されて (sarete) is simply the て-form of される, which is the passive form of する (to do). Because されて looks like: さ (one syllable) れて (another syllable group), learners sometimes think it might be two words. But grammatically, it's one verb form.
Breakdown:
- する = to do
- される = to be done (passive)
- されて = being done / having been done (て-form)

You see it most often in phrases like:
Shin'yō sarete iru / 信用されている
= "is trusted" / "is being trusted"

Appendix B offers a small glimpse of what could grow into a future project: a full vocabulary companion containing hundreds of Japanese words, each explored with the same depth and sentence-level analysis shown here. If you have thoughts or suggestions, I welcome them at X: @EdgarJHern12748.

CLOSING THOUGHTS

Learning Japanese is not just about memorizing vocabulary or mastering verb charts. It's about understanding how people actually speak, how they soften a statement, emphasize a feeling, hesitate, reflect, connect ideas, or reveal emotion through the smallest particles and stems. These subtle choices are the heartbeat of natural Japanese, and by working through this book, you've taken a step that many learners never take.

If you've reached this point, you've done more than study grammar. You've trained your ear. You've sharpened your intuition. You've learned to notice the difference between what is correct and what is natural. That awareness will stay with you long after the details fade, and it will continue to grow each time you listen, read, or speak.

Remember that nuance is not something you "finish." It's something you grow into. Every conversation, every sentence you encounter, will reinforce what you've learned here. Keep paying attention. Keep listening for tone, intention, and feeling. The stems and patterns in this book are not rules to memorize, they are tools to help you understand people.

As you continue your journey, be patient with yourself. Celebrate small breakthroughs. And above all, enjoy the process. Japanese is a language of subtlety, warmth, and depth. You now have the foundation to appreciate it in a way that few beginners ever do.

Thank you for letting this book be part of your learning.
Your journey doesn't end here; it opens from here.

Coming Soon from Clarity House Publications:
Kanji By Imagination: A Fun, Visual Method for Remembering Kanji
(The companion volume to Japanese Stems & Nuances)
Also look for the Spanish version.

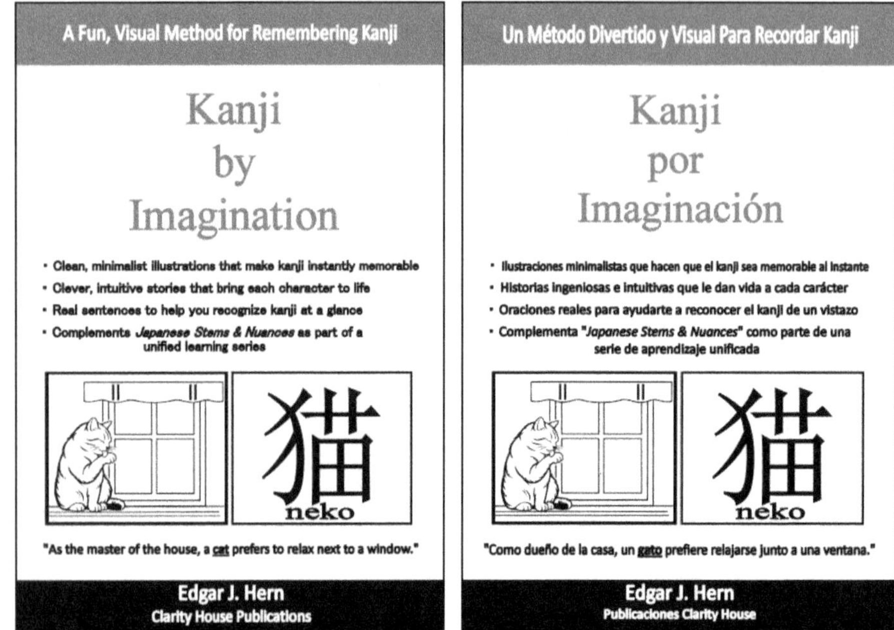

www.ingramcontent.com/pod-product-compliance
Lightning Source LLC
LaVergne TN
LVHW081316110826
845149LV00006B/1523

* 9 7 9 8 9 9 5 4 6 8 5 0 9 *